D1062783

The West of Ireland

by the same author

Poems
Always Adam
The Cloth of Flesh

Biography
Pioneers in Printing

Translations
Beloved Son Felix
Journal of a Younger Brother

Travel
Munster
Connacht
Deserts of England
The Pilgrims' Way
Paris
The Loire
Cork and Kerry
The Ridgeway Path
The South Downs Way

Technical
The Making of Books

SEÁN JENNETT

The West
of Ireland

W. W. Norton & Co. Inc.
New York

DEER PARK PUBLIC LIBRARY
44 LAKE AVENUE
DEER PARK, N. Y. 11729

First published 1980
Copyright © Seán Jennett 1980

First American Edition 1980
All Rights Reserved
0-393-01338-3
Printed in Great Britain

Contents

Acknowledgement *vi*

List of illustrations *vii*

Map *viii*

Introduction *1*

1 County Clare *6*

2 South County Galway *26*

3 Loch Corrib and East County Galway *40*

4 The City of Galway *50*

5 The Aran Islands *55*

6 Iar-Chonnacht and Connemara *64*

7 South County Mayo *103*

8 North County Mayo *115*

9 County Sligo *129*

The meaning of Irish place-names *143*

Bibliography *145*

Index *147*

Acknowledgement

In the preparation of this book I owe a great deal to more persons than I can name, but in particular I owe thanks to Bord Fáilte for its unmatched information service and its unfailing readiness to answer questions and to solve problems that were often difficult. I am grateful to Mr. Terence J. Sheehy for reading the typescript and correcting several errors. My wife Irene accompanied me on my journeys in Ireland, kept a record of our wanderings, and noted divergent spellings of place-names. She also typed the final draft of the book.

The description of the Pietà at Strade first appeared in an article in *Country Life*.

List of Illustrations

Between pages 70–86

1 Yeat's Thoor Ballylee
2 The Corrib valley
3 Lynch's castle
4 Aran Islanders at Inishmaan
5 Carved capital at Cong
6 Aughananure castle
7 Entrance to Dún Aengus
8 Loch Nafooey
9–12 Irish cottages
13 Summit of Croagh Patrick
14 Mountain pass near Loch Fee
15 Doonbristy
16 Fishing in Sligo town
17 A turbary with turves drying

18 Parke's Castle
19 Stones of the west
20 Entrance gable of Creeragh
      church
21 Gathering seaweed at
      Bertraboy Bay
22 Roundstone harbour
23 Kildavnet castle
24 Stone circle at Carrowmore
25 Enniscrone
26 Ballintubber abbey
27 Flamboyant tracery at Strade
28 The Pietà at Strade

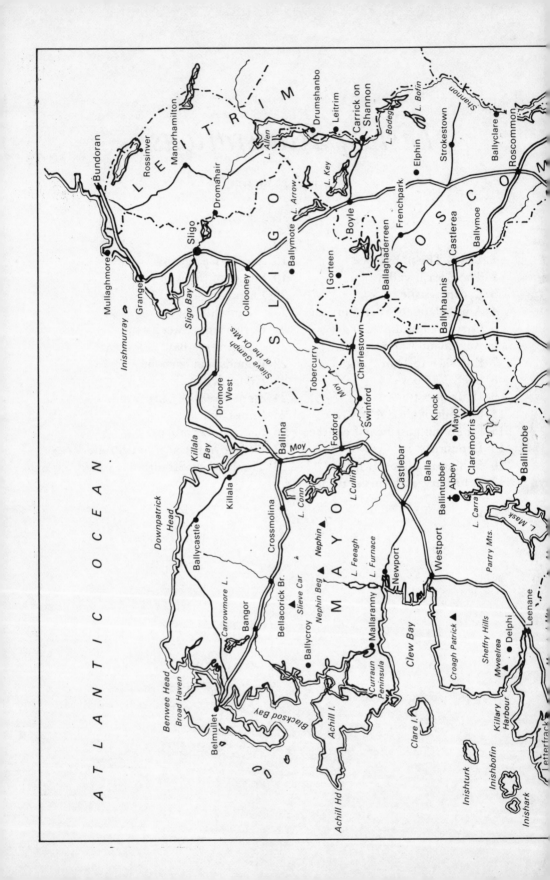

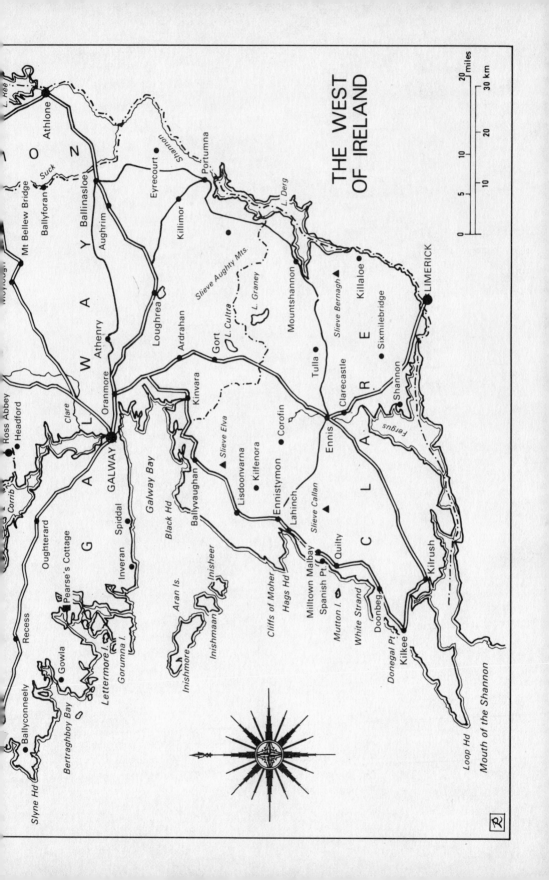

THE WEST
OF IRELAND

Introduction

The west of Ireland, you may suppose, must be a distinct area, since it is not only the subject of this book but has been the subject of several others. It is as distinct an area as the West Country of England or the Old West of America. Everybody knows where those are, of course. But put a crayon into a man's hand and bid him delineate one of them and a doubt is at once apparent. Nobody is quite certain where the boundaries should be drawn. In Ireland our puzzled subject, set before a map of the whole country, could with two lines divide the island into four and with a modicum of knowledge of its history he would have divided it into its historical provinces – Leinster to the east, Munster to the south, Ulster to the north, and Connacht to the west.

Would this western quarter be THE west? It would include too much for some people, too much land that does not have the character of what it is supposed the west should be. The west is something else. Mere tribal divisions or political divisions will not do. They do not take sufficient account of the character, that is, the geography and geology of the land, or even of the colour of the sea and of the lakes, nor of speech or customs, or of the manner of the people who live in and are the west. The rising sun in the morning and the declining sun in the evening – especially the declining sun – seem to condition the hearts and minds of those who dwell in the west, as though it must be the declining sun that is responsible for the melancholy they are supposed to display – though I have found plenty of humour and even of rumbustious laughter in the people of the west.

How then can we delineate them, draw a ring round them and say *that* is where they are, *that* is their country? It has been done for us, Nature has set a moat round them, and the moat is the mighty Shannon, which begins near the northern limits of the west and as a great river studded with lakes along its course, partitions off six counties, counties that I submit are the veritable west. The counties are Clare, Galway, Mayo, and Sligo, with bits of Leitrim and Roscommon that do not matter in our argument. It is co-incidental that in Galway, Mayo, and Sligo these counties of the west include a large part of the province of Connacht, while Clare is one of the six counties of Munster. They have between them common characteristics that unite them. Important is their grouping within the line of the Shannon, and also the fact that they all face the strong and turbulent Atlantic. They are as one island within an island, facing towards two thousand miles of ocean.

For long the west was remote and far from the centre of power and European and English culture. It was desperately poor, with its people living in large part on land that was agriculturally and therefore economically almost barren. This, with political disadvantages imposed by English overlords as a result of rebellions and risings, with consequent repression, locked the people as tenants in their own land in a state of subsistence economy that was self-perpetuating.

The Irish Language

The isolation of the people in simple agriculture was an important factor in the survival of the old Irish language, Gaelic (which some people, mostly non-Irish, like to call Erse). Until the famine of the 1840s, when the principal subsistence food, potatoes, repeatedly failed, Gaelic was the common language of most of the population. But the effect of the famine was principally felt by the poorest levels of the population, as famines generally are, and these were the classes in which Gaelic had its strongest hold. These people died by the thousand, and those who could gather money enough to escape the country and save their lives emigrated. The population was reduced by millions and the strength of Irish as a spoken language was greatly reduced.

The language survives in the west, in many places in the mountains and along the coast and in the islands, and it now has the advantage of encouragement by the government. But it is now for ever a minority language and it is, despite what its enthusiasts may claim, probably in decline.

Most speakers of Irish are bilingual and it is probable that, though you may hear Irish spoken in many places, you will not meet anyone who does not speak English. There are, however, still many people for whom English is a second language, spoken with conscious effort, as though the speaker were translating from his native Irish. This 'imperfection' of English speech – if you like to call it that – this carry-over of Irish idiom into English, brings about an extraordinarily attractive and expressive kind of English that is very different from English English. I am not speaking of accent, what the English understand by the term 'brogue'. Irish English attracted the attention of notable writers and it may be studied best, if slightly idealised, in the plays of John Millington Synge and Lady Augusta Gregory, such as *Riders to the Sea* of the one and *The Rising of the Moon* of the other.

As a literary language Irish in the vernacular or in translation has many triumphs, but it is in the nature of the response to changing modern needs that the persistence of a language has to be measured, the need and ability to express the concepts of science and of mechanics, and here the response is not encouraging.

Irish is, nevertheless, a very beautiful language, rich in poetic concept and musical in sound. You may hear it spoken especially along the west coast and on the islands, as on Aran, and on such peninsulas as Loop Head. In places, as at Spiddal in Galway, in Sligo, and at Carrigaholt in Clare, there are colleges of Irish, where students may come to learn and practice the language in the company of native speakers, that is, of those who were born to Irish and learned it at their mother's knee. Facility in the language may be indicated by a small, plain ring, the *fáinne*, worn by students in the lapel or as a brooch – a gold ring for the expert, a silver one for those less so.

In the republic you may see Irish on signposts and road signs, where the Irish and English versions of names are given one below the other. It also appears in many books and also in newspapers, which, however, usually print only a column or two in the language.

Land divisions

There are many land divisions that have names but may not have boundaries on the map. Among these are ancient baronies, whose names are still in use as though the baronies continued to exist, though they have not existed these hundreds of years. Such are Murrisk and Erris and Tirawley, and Ballynahinch, Kilconnel and Kiltartan. Then there are other divisions without fixed margins, which may or may not include whole baronies. There is, for example, Joyce's Country, which is in the mountains west of Loch Mask, and Iar-Chonnact (that is West Connacht), which is the hill country of granite inland from the coastal road west of Galway town; and Cois Fhairrge, which means 'beside the sea' and denotes part of the coast north of Galway Bay. And there is Connemara, the famous Connemara, whose name has been taken to cover everything west of Galway and Loch Corrib round to Murrisk and Westport. The name of Connemara is, more narrowly, used for the country of mountains and fretted coast between the Maumturks and Aughrus Point, between Roundstone and Killary Harbour.

Yet another name likely to puzzle the visitor is that of the Gaeltacht. 'The Gaeltacht' is a general name for all those parts of Ireland where Gaelic, or Irish, is spoken. It is used in opposition to a less frequent term, the Galltacht, the districts where English is the reigning language. 'Gall' means stranger or foreigner.

The stone beneath

In the east of our district, towards the Shannon and beyond the river, lies the limestone of the plain, which extends to the strange uplands of the Burren in county Clare and includes the Aran islands in Galway Bay, and in the north, in county Sligo, rears the spectacular tabular mountains of Ben Bulben and its neighbours.

Between the two and forming the hard fist of the far west, thrust in the face of the Atlantic, rise the soaring ranges of the mountains, formed mostly of resistant igneous or intrusive or metamorphic rocks – of quartzite and granite for the Maumturks and the Twelve Bens, of Ordovician shales for Mweelrea and the Sheeffry Hills, of quartzite again for Nephin Beag and the isolated Croagh Patrick, of schist and gneiss and granite for the Ox Mountains, which extend through county Sligo to Loch Gill. The geological map of this area is a patchwork of coloured shreds, divided in the south by the long waters of Loch Corrib and Loch Mask from the pale blue by which geologists indicate limestone.

Not that you will easily see the surface of all these rocks. The naked bone is clothed almost everywhere with the flesh of verdure, of grass and of woodland and of bog; but here and there the bone is bare, as it is in the Burren of Clare and on the quartzite of summits such as Croagh Patrick and Nephin. For the difference between the rocks look to the plants. Where the limestone is not overlain by centuries of acid bog calcicole or lime-loving plants will flourish, as they do notably in the Burren. There a remarkable flora has developed on the harsh *karst* slopes and terraces of the limestone. The harder rocks of the mountains, less well drained, tend to produce an acid flora, often highly interesting but different.

The people

The frequently unwelcoming and inhospitable shores and uplands of the west nevertheless attracted populations from early times. They were the people who came to Ireland generally for rich farmlands, but one might like to suppose that those who pressed on or were driven to the coasts and the mountains came first because of the intense beauty of the landscape, with its capes and promontories, its islands and its cliffs and the hazy polychrome of its ranges of mountains, which caught their breath with beauty and made other considerations a secondary matter. The invading peoples flowed in and over the plains and the valleys and fought for their possession, peoples shadowy in legends that date perhaps from the bronze age. The stories tell of Fomorians and Nemedians in times far distant, of the small, dark Fir Bolg – the men of the bags, who are said to have come from Greece and may have been the Belgae – of the tall, fair De Danaan, who were magical, every one a wizard, but were none the less defeated by the Milesians from Spain. Notable battles took place, so it is said, on the plains of Mayo and Moytura. The blood of these distant peoples flows in the veins of the modern Irishman, together with that of Norman, Welsh, and English. The romantic or patriotic Irishman who occasionally calls himself a Celt or a Gael is certainly as different from the Englishman as the Basque and the Catalan are from the Spaniard. He is nevertheless a mongrel. As, I do not doubt, are all the other races of the earth – including the Englishman, who is largely of Irish descent.

1
County Clare

Clare, the ancient kingdom of Thomond, though by no means unknown, has never achieved a fame among tourists equivalent to that of Kerry or of Galway. Tourists tend to treat Clare as an interruption between the renowned places of Killarney (and lately of the Dingle peninsula) and the glories of Connemara. True, Clare does not have mountains to match those of Kerry and Galway, but it has lakes arguably as beautiful as anything in Ireland. It has much interesting and attractive countryside, many fine antiquities, and in the cliffs of Moher spectacle as astounding as the visitor could wish for. And then there is the Burren. Queer country indeed, with its harsh grey limestone *karst* landscapes, not offering much to the hasty passer-by but wonderfully rewarding for those who have the patience and time for more leisurely examination.

You may guess by this that Clare has been neglected. It has indeed, so much so that until not so long ago one might have had the illusion of travelling in touristically virgin country. It is getting to be better known, as it deserves to be, but it is still very far from being tourist-ridden.

One of the reasons why, even today, Clare remains comparatively isolated is that it is still defended by the great breadth of the Shannon. Its neighbour in the south is county Kerry, but Kerry is on the other side of the estuary of the Shannon, separated by several miles of salt water, with only the fairly recent car ferry from Tarbert to Killimer to link them. Until that came into being the traveller had to go inland almost to the centre of Ireland (Birr is reputed the true centre) to find a bridge across the river. That bridge is at Limerick, one of the major cities of Ireland, larger than anything we are going to find in the west. Upstream from Limerick there are other bridges – O Brien's Bridge, where Cromwell and Ireton forced a crossing in 1653; and at Killaloe, which was the headquarters of the Dalcassian kings of Munster, who with Brian Boru, became high kings of Ireland. The Dalcassians were the O Brien's, who remained a power in this land of Clare and whose name we shall encounter frequently throughout the county.

Killaloe and Ennis

Killaloe, the church of St. Lua, owes its name to St. Lua or Molua, who founded a church and monastery here in the sixth century. The town, with its bridge of thirteen arches, stands at the foot of the beautiful Loch Derg, which is threaded by the current of the river Shannon, and its site was consequently of obvious strategic value. The O Briens were here before the tenth century in the person of St. Flannan, who was then governing the monastery. His delightful little oratory, with its amazingly steep Celtic roof, stands next to the cathedral, and equally amazing, after all these centuries, is the fact that it is still complete. It has a romanesque west doorway, with the arch resting on two carved capitals, but few windows, and the interior is dark and gloomy. This is not unusual, even among a people noted for their love of books and their delight in making them, and suggests their difficulty in making windows that would keep the weather out and let the light in.

The cathedral of St. Flannan has since the reformation been the cathedral of the Protestant diocese. The Catholic see is at Ennis. The cathedral of St. Flannan is said to have been built by Dónal Mór O Brien in the twelfth century on the site of an earlier cathedral. It has evidently undergone considerable restoration at various times, with a restoration in the nineteenth century that has left its unmistakable mark.

In the south-west corner of the interior is an interesting group of antique pieces that stand distinct from the nineteenth-century cathedral. Set in the wall is what was once an exterior doorway, very sumptuous romanesque, almost barbaric, with four orders of arches all richly carved, as also are the shafts. This rich and ancient doorway may possibly be the very doorway of the cathedral built by Dónal Mór O Brien. The sill of the doorway is composed of two inscribed stones, one of which is a gravestone and the other part of a cross. In front of the doorway and separate from it is a low stone that is part of another ancient cross, with inscriptions both in ogham and in runes, a very rare combination. They say 'Thorgrimr carved this cross' and 'A blessing upon Thorgrimr'. On the opposite face of the stone is a roughly carved cross. Thorgrimr may have been a Christianised Viking who carved his name and his blessing about the year 1000. His personality seems still to imbue the atmosphere as of some old ghost. Nearby is a font said to be eighteenth century but looking considerably older. Still in this corner, stands an elaborately carved high cross, with knotwork and fret patterns and a robed figure of Christ. This cross originally stood in Kilfenora, a place of high crosses, as we shall see. It was moved to Killaloe in 1821 and probably dates from the twelfth century.

The Roman Catholic church stands on a hill at the top of this hilly town, on what is said to have been and very likely was the site of Brian Boru's palace of Kincora, lamented by the poets. Brian Boru was the greatest of the Dalcassian kings, who extended his sway from Munster to the whole of Ireland and might have made Ireland a truly independent and united nation. He was killed in his hour of victory over the Norse at Clontarf near Dublin by a Norse warrior who had strayed from the battle and probably could not believe his luck at finding the old king at his mercy. The year was 1014.

The Catholic church is a modern building, with a beautiful stained-glass window by Harry Clarke. In the churchyard stands St. Molua's oratory, a little, ruined Celtic church that originally stood on Friar's Island in the Shannon. It was rebuilt here in 1930 when the island was submerged in the hydro-electric scheme that provided a great deal of the country with power.

Crossing the Shannon at Limerick, between King John's castle and the Treaty Stone, does not bring you immediately into county Clare. You still have a mile or two to go on the Tll, which is the Ennis road, before you actually enter county Clare.

At Cratloe the road passes between the river and Woodcock Hill, which at 1010 feet represents the southern end of the Slieve Barnagh range. On the slope of the hill are Cratloe Woods, which were once so notable for their great oaks that Richard II cut timber here to help re-roof Westminster Hall. That magnificent roof, which is said to weigh 660 tons, with timbers a yard through and 21 feet long, must have required the finest and largest oaks that could be found and compelled the builders to search far for them, even to the shores of the Shannon.

A few miles farther west, on the Newmarket road, rises the splendid tower-house of Bunratty, among the largest of its kind and comparable with that at Blarney near Cork. It stands beside a small stone bridge over a shallow river and dwarfs the bridge and the two-storey public house that faces it. The river is a tributary of the Shannon and, despite its modest size, boasts three names. It is the Ratty, the O Garney, and the Owenogarney. The last is merely another way of saying 'river O

Garney', 'owen' being the Irish word 'abhainn', which is familiar in English place-names as 'avon'. The present castle is at least the fourth on this site, the first having been built by a Norman knight called Robert de Muscegrow. It was probably of timber, perhaps from those woods of Cratloe we have already noticed. A stone castle was built in 1227 by Thomas de Clare, who had English colonists established here, to protect his property. These could not stop the Irish, who rightly saw the castle as a threat, from destroying it twice within a few years. It next came into the hands of Sir Thomas Rokeby, the king's justiciar, who lost it in 1353 to the warring Irish. The present castle was built about 1450 by Maccon Mac Sioda Mac Conmara and completed by his son Seán Finn in 1467. By the year 1500 the castle was once again in the possession of the O Briens, who thenceforth held it until the Civil War, when they allowed it to be occupied by the Parliamentarian Admiral Penn, the father of William Penn, the founder of Pennsylvania.

The castle had several subsequent owners until it was bought as a ruin in 1954 by Lord Gort. Lord Gort, in conjunction with the Office of Public Works and Bord Fáilte, restored it and opened it to the public, with its fine rooms furnished with a remarkable collection of antiques of the fourteenth to the fifteenth centuries.

Today Bunratty is one of the brightest highlights of the tourist route through Clare – providing a memorable setting for one of those medieval banquets for which Ireland is well known and which have been copied elsewhere.

Bunratty is a great square fortress with projecting turrets at the corners linked by arches near the roof. The parapets are boldly battlemented in the Irish fashion. It is five storeys high, with a basement below, and a large banqueting hall and a great hall above, from which opens a small chapel. In the banqueting hall guests eat and drink in medieval fashion and listen to Irish music of appropriate periods.

In 1959 work on the extension of Shannon airport necessitated the re-moval of an old Mac Namara farmhouse and to preserve it this building was re-erected near the castle. It was followed by other cottages and farm-houses and now there exists a folk park, which preserves various kinds of farmhouses and cottages and suitable industries such as a forge. The grouping of these buildings in the shadow of the great tower-house suggests the houses that are known to have existed here in the days of the de Clares.

A little to the west by the Shannon, at Rinneanna, is the great Shannon airport and its associated shopping and trading complex.

From this airport you may fly afar, and if you wish you may go loaded down with booty like a successful robber. And like a robber you will not have to pay excise tax on what you carry away. Here you may buy anything from automobiles to cameras, from jewels to watches, at the large duty-free shopping complex. The only condition you must meet is that you make arrangements to send your goods abroad, or take them with you on your plane. You need not have stayed in Ireland longer than to transfer from one plane to another.

The Shannon area has been connected with air transport for many years. A little way downstream, at Foynes in Limerick, between the wars, there used to be a seaplane terminus, once well known.

At Foynes, in the river, is Aughinish Island, with the remains of a castle. Here Alcan, the big aluminium combine, in June 1978 initiated a large alumina manufacturing plant that is expected to cost £287 million. This plant will be, as it were, only a staging point. The basic material, bauxite, will be imported from Guinea and South America, and the manufactured aluminium will be exported.

Newmarket on Fergus, north of the airport, takes its name from a nineteenth-century O Brien – Lord Inchiquin – who was overwhelmingly enthusiastic about horses and horse-racing, and meant to have a place on his estate with the same name as the racing centre in England.

Inchiquin's castle of Dromoland stands in a fine demesne off the Ennis road farther north. There was a medieval castle or tower-house here, but in 1830 Lord Inchiquin commissioned the architects James and George Richard Pain to build him a new neo-gothic mansion. They produced a huge and handsome and romantic building that still stands, though today it is an hotel of a luxury kind.

Facing the entrance to the grounds on the opposite side of the road stands a small, classical belvedere or gazebo. It was built by Lord Inchiquin as a viewpoint for the horse-races that were his chief interest.

An ornamental gateway in the grounds was once the entrance to the former O Brien castle of Leamaneh, which we shall come to in due course. Also in the grounds – the Irish almost invariably use the term 'demesne' for such grounds – is Mooghaun, the largest stone ring-fort in Ireland. It is trivallate, ie with three concentric banks and ditches encircling the top of a hill, and measures about 1500 feet by 1000 feet. It is probably a little over two thousand years old.

It was perhaps the people from this fort who buried a huge collection of gold ornaments and vessels east of Dromoland. It came to light in 1854, when workmen stumbled on it during the digging and construction of the railway line to Ennis. The workmen may not have recognised the gold immediately, but they knew they had come upon something interesting and old and it was gathered up at once and dispersed among them. But they soon knew the great Clare gold find for what it was. Despite the quantity – it is said to have been the largest hoard of prehistoric gold ornaments found in Europe – most of it disappeared, probably disposed of to dealers, who melted it down. A few pieces found their way into the national Museum in Dublin, where intensely beautiful examples shine in glass cases and give some idea of what the Great Clare Gold Find was like. The cottages and houses of the district have been combed again and again since then by collectors and dealers hoping to discover something left over from the find. There is a story that on a farm once a boy found what his father thought was a brass coffin handle, and which he threw into a bush as rubbish. Later he showed it to an archæologist, who recognised it as a Celtic gold torque. The story is enough to inspire the searchers.

The iron age is experienced again at Craiganowen near Sixmilebridge. The Craiganowen project comprises principally a reconstruction of a crannóg dwelling and a restored tower-house used as a museum. There is also a more extensive museum, but that is farther away and not in Clare – it is at Plassey House in Limerick.

A crannóg is a fortified dwelling on an island, usually an artificial island made of logs and brushwood – 'crann' is the Irish for tree. It was usually built just a short distance from the shore, with which it was connected by a timber bridge or a causeway. The crannóg at Craiganowen, entirely modern in construction, is based on good archæological evidence – there are remains of crannógs in various parts of Ireland. Craiganowen's crannóg comprises a small round island surrounded by a stockade of posts joined by wattle, with a raised watchtower of timber and wattle over the entrance from the bridge. On the island are two heavily thatched huts, one rectangular and the other round. This represents a family dwelling of the iron age, and may be compared with the iron-age village constructed on Butser Hill in the south of England, and with the BBC's experimental project in Dorset, which formed the subject of a series of television programmes. The houses at Craiganowen are furnished with replicas of bronze-age or iron-age implements and utensils.

The crannóg may be compared with the ring fort, of which there are literally thousands in Ireland. The smaller ring-forts were clearly family dwellings, surrounded by a wall or bank of stones or earth to give protection to domestic animals, but some forts were more evidently military or defensive in character, as seems to have been the case with the enormous trivallate fort at Mooaughn.

Ring-forts often contain one or more souterrains. These underground chambers were built to give temporary refuge for the family in times of danger. There is a souterrain under the ring-fort at Craiganowen.

It is evident even from these simple defences that Ireland in the bronze age and in the iron age was not always peaceful, and in this it differed little from other places of these periods.

Warring tribes and interloping nations made it no safer in the middle ages, and the large numbers of tower-houses dotting the countryside are evidence of the turmoil that was always feared. A tower-house was the home of the local chief or lord, who usually had retainers on the lower floors and his own hall and bed-chamber above. Many tower-houses are very small, and must have been no more than watch-towers, with a small garrison, but others were more distinctly dwellings, though very constricted and crowded. The Craiganowen castle was built by the Mac Namaras about 1550 and was destroyed about the middle of the seventeenth century. It was restored at various periods after 1820 and was inhabited. It is now a museum.

Off the Quin road stands Knappogue, another castle of the Mac Namaras, built by Síoda Mac Namara, who completed Bunratty, which his father had begun in 1433. Knappogue was occupied and damaged by the Parliamentarians, but subsequently it had a long history of occupation by owners or tenants until it was bought by a Texan American and his wife. In conjunction with the Shannon Free Development Airport Company and Bord Fáilte, it was restored as a centre for medieval banquets and entertainments. The old tower-house, with its small, defensive windows, has a lower extension of about 1800 with larger Georgian windows that are distinctive.

At the next crossroads a right turn leads to Quin abbey, which, as one of the best preserved monastic ruins in Ireland, is frequently visited by coach parties on sight-seeing tours. This abbey is also a foundation of Síoda Mac Namara's, incorporating the remains of a castle built by de Clare in 1280. The remnants of the square towers of this castle can be made out in the abbey walls.

The abbey was founded for Franciscans, whose architectural taste and handiwork can be seen in the well preserved cloisters and the tracery of the windows. The abbey was suppressed in 1541 – or at least that was the intention of the Reformation; but the monks were not easily daunted and there were Franciscans at Quinn until the nineteenth century, the last of them being buried in the cloister. His occupation of a grave in that position was a last defiance.

The abbey is roofless, but much of the conventual plan remains, with the dormitory over the cloisters. The high and graceful central tower is notable.

Beyond a stream near the abbey is St. Finghin's church, built between 1278 and 1285, except for the belfry, which is later.

Ennis stands on the river Fergus, a rapid little river where it passes below the bridges in the town, but one that soon develops into a broad estuary scattered with islands where it joins the Shannon above Foynes. The streets are narrow and winding and deliver the visitor to a central junction, where there rises Ennis's principal modern monument, a classical column in memory of Daniel O Connell. He was a notable orator and was member for Clare in the Westminster Parliament from 1828 to 1831. A mass meeting was held here in 1828 to nominate O Connell for the seat, even though the repressive laws of the time disqualified Catholics, and O Connell was a Catholic. But he won the election with such a resounding majority that it was obvious even to the die-hard Protestants of Parliament that he could not be kept out.

A friend of O Connell's, Tom Steele, is commemorated near the river in Newbridge Road, by a rock carved with a shield bearing an emblem of a rampart lion. Steele is remembered for his persistent love of a lady, a Miss Crow. Tom fell enamoured of her and would sit for hours on the rock looking at her house and hoping to win her heart and take her home to his farm at Tulla. But Miss Crow would have none of him and, apparently faithful to the last, he died a bachelor.

Miss Crow's house eventually became the Gárda station, and it was here I had to go to collect the key of what is called Ennis abbey, but which in fact was a Franciscan friary, founded by Donchadh Cairbreach O Brien, King of Thomond, just before his death in 1242. It was subsequently very much changed at various periods up to the fifteenth century. The friary is roofless now and partly in ruin, but in a corner of the nave of the church St. Francis rules his adherents still in the guise of a jolly little figure raising his hands palm upwards to show the stigmata.

There are other interesting carvings in this friary, notably in the chancel. There, two beautiful tombs stand beneath the sky and are consequently less protected than they should be. The more easterly one was erected about 1460 for a Mac Mahon and carries a series of panels showing the life of Christ in costumes that appear in style to date from the twelfth century onwards. On the back wall of the tomb are thirteen figures of the Apostles with Christ.

West of the Mac Mahon tomb is another that has interesting ogee crocketed canopies, and in one of the arches of this is a screen of flamboyant pierced tracery.

Ennis is, of course, the county town of Clare, which is the reason for the classical court-house, and it is also the Catholic see, with a cathedral.

There is much of interest in the district, including scenery which is both remarkable and wonderful.

Leaving Ennis in the morning we followed the L53 north and turned off on a lesser road to Dysert O Déa. The name means 'O Déa's hermitage', but the place is known also for another saint, called Tola, who was here in the eighth century. It is a site full of atmosphere, with a presence that permeates and makes one a little uneasy, as though you might at any moment be caught trespassing.

Is it all the centuries of prayer that have passed here, or the noise and clash of the battle that drove back the Normans in 1318 and killed de Clare of Bunratty, or is it the fact that everything, all the antiquities here, are in ruin? One of the oldest things in sight, a high cross called the White Cross of Tola, is the most complete. It stands on a green rise, a low hill, on a pedestal plinth, and belongs to the twelfth century. On the cross are inscriptions recording that it was repaired in 1683 and was re-erected in 1871 by Redwood Synge and his wife, who built and lived in the house now ruined among the trees by the roadside. The high cross is richly carved. On the west side Christ is shown in a pleated robe, and below him is a bishop with a crozier, both figures in high relief. The bishop was originally intended to project still more, with an arm inserted in a socket. The east side of the cross has panels of intricate zoomorphic pattern, the north has figures, and the south has more ornament. Below the cross is the stump of a round tower, with its base built of enormous stones which suggest an early origin. The door, as was usual with round towers, was high off the ground, to make access difficult for intruders.

Near the tower stands a roofless church, of romanesque character, with a richly carved south doorway, which may have been altered or may be a compound of two doorways. It has four orders, all sumptuously carved, the nook shafts having spirals and zig-zags and the arch a fascinating row of facial masks.

There seems to be no life at Dysert now, but how busy it must have been in its day!

Corofin, to the north, stands in a country of lakes and is a great place for fishermen, for trout and coarse fish. The fishermen have the benefit of very pretty scenery, especially around Loch Inchiquin, on the north shore of which rises the roofless Inchiquin castle, built in 1459 for the O Briens.

North again, near Roughan, we found one of the most curious things in Ireland. It is the Tau cross of Killinaboy. 'Killinaboy' comes from the Irish Cill Inghine Baoithe, which means 'the church of Sister Baoith', presumably a nun. There is a ruin of an early church of little interest except for a carving of a shiela-na-gig over the door – a shiela-na-gig is an erotic female figure, usually ugly and contorted, often found on old churches but having no obvious religious connection. This one is worn and not clearly made out. There is also the stump of a round tower and a ruined tower-house retaining part of its surrounding bawn; it is called de Clare's house.

The Tau cross is at Roughan which, if you have to ask your direction, will be more readily understood if you pronounce it in the Irish way – 'Ru'an'. There is nothing to be seen here but a Bord Fáilte sign pointing to a stile in the wall, and just inside the field we found the thing we were looking for. The cross is only about two feet high and it is not really a cross. It is rather a letter T with the arms slightly raised as though it meant to be a Y. The two arms are carved as two heads joined at the neck and glumly looking at the sky. There is nothing else like it in Ireland, but similar carved stones have been found at Roquepertuse in France. It is difficult to imagine what Christian purpose could have been served by this monument at Crossineenboy, and it is likely that it is pre-Christian.

Set here in the lonely countryside, gazing forever at the clouds, it seems to have an air of incomprehensible menace.

The main road, the L53, leading to Kilfenora, is known as Sir Donat's Road. Sir Donat O Brien was the owner of Leamaneh castle, which we found standing a little off the road, a noble house illustrating the transition from grim tower-house to mansion. Though joined in one, the two parts are quite distinct. The tower was larger and stronger than many tower-houses are, and with its slit-like loops suitable for guns it was obviously defensive, an impression re-inforced by the corner bartizans and the remains of the bawn that once surrounded it and which can still be traced. The castle retains its stone vault supporting the top floor. In 1643 Conor O Brien added a four-storey mansion with large mullioned windows, larger than the original castle. Conor O Brien was killed in a battle with Cromwellians. His redoubtable wife Máire Ní Mahan, or Máire Ruadh ('Red Mary') immediately set off for Limerick, where she married a Cromwellian soldier, for by that means she could prevent the expropriation of her land by the Cromwellians and preserve her heritage for her son Donat. The soldier, called Cooper, was of little more use to her than this, and one day she pushed him out of a window of the castle when he made some unfortunate remark about her first husband.

Donat or Donough O Brien, as it turned out, was hanged in 1582.

There used to be an ornate gateway to the castle, but this was removed in the nineteenth century to that other O Brien castle of Dromoland, as I have already mentioned.

Kilfenora has a display centre providing information about the remarkable tract of land known as the Burren, of which it was reported to Cromwell that it had not any tree to hang a man, nor enough water to drown him, nor enough earth to bury him. The Burren stretches north to Galway Bay, west to the Atlantic, east towards the Galway border. But before we go on to consider the Burren we ought certainly to pause and explore the village of Kilfenora. It is full of charm and naïve antiquity, a little place in which the grey of the stone of the buildings and the grey of the stony landscape seem to marry with the sunlight in pellucid air. The tiny village was the see of a bishop from the twelfth century and possibly earlier, for the office may have originated in a monastery founded by St. Fachtna. The twelfth-century church is still called the cathedral, and it still has a bishop, who is, would you believe it, the Pope!

The cathedral is divided into two by a wall. The western half is roofed and is still used for divine service. It contains little of antiquarian interest. The eastern portion, the chancel, is open to the sky and is full of interest. The beautiful east window has three round-headed lancets. These accord with the date of the twelfth century, to which much else in Kilfenora belongs. In the corner on each side of the window there is a crude effigy of a bishop. One of these is said to represent St. Fachna, to whom the cathedral is dedicated. In the north wall is a beautiful pointed tomb recess of Decorated design, which was perhaps used as an Easter sepulchre. It has been described as a triple sedilia, but if it is it must have accommodated priests with very narrow rumps. West of this is a doorway and next to that is a slab with an incised figure of a bishop.

To understand the profusion of high crosses at Kilfenora you must see in your mind's eye an episcopal procession emerging from the church in full panoply and pomp. There would be monks and priests, and the bishop in his vestments with his crozier, as shown on the carvings. He would be preceded by small boys swinging censers and creating a blue haze of incense. Perhaps they would pause and gather round the high crosses in turn and recite a mass or two. But why so many crosses? There are three in the churchyard and another in a field near by. And we must remember the high cross in the cathedral at Killaloe, which was originally at Kilfenora. They all come from the twelfth century. The thing is that a high cross is a prayer enunciated in stone, and you cannot have too many prayers, now can you?

The first cross we notice, in the churchyard near the path, has a curious carving of a bishop and two other figures arm in arm. The second cross, to the north, has pattern carving. The third is a stump. The high cross west of the village, in a field, is thirteen feet high and is also twelfth-century. On it is a figure of Christ and a pattern of ropes.

Caherballykinvarga, two miles north-east, is not easy to find and some inquiry may be necessary. 'Cathair' means a fort and specifically a stone fort (*lios*, pronounce *liss*, is the word for a fort with earthen banks). Caherballykinvarga is a round fort on a hill, and is very much ruined. Many forts may have been no more than farm or domestic enclosures, but Caherballykinvarga was distinctly military and defensive, for it has a feature that is remarkable and unusual and which you will not see again until you come to examine the great fort of Dún Aonghus on Inishmore on the Aran islands. This feature is called a *chevaux de frise*. It consists of sharp spars of stone set close together and upright in the ground, in the manner of a tank-trap. Try to pick your way through this while keeping an eye open for missiles emanating from the fort, but if you crack your shins or your ankles remember you have been warned!

Another fort that appears definitely military is Cahercommaun. It has three concentric walls, with one of the circles incomplete on a cliff edge. It was dangerous when it was built and it is dangerous still.

At Kilfenora we turned off southwards towards Ennistimon. This is a small market town on the river Cullenagh, two and a half miles from Liscannor Bay on the west coast. A ruined eighteenth-century church stands prominently in the midst of a veritable *chevaux de frise* of gravestones. We stood on a bridge and looked down at the river below rushing and sliding over slabs of rock, spectacular and vertiginous. West of the bridge is a modern (1953) Catholic church, with a tall thin tower, which I mention because it contains notable stations of the Cross by Father Aengus Buckley, which I would like you to see. Look out for such modern little Catholic churches, and look especially at the stations and at the stained glass. There are some very worthwhile surprises. There are some disappointments too, as where an admirable and sensitive design has been harmed by the introduction of the familiar and aesthetically atrocious figures of Our Lady and Bleeding Hearts of Victorian inspiration.

Lisdoonvara, north of Ennistimon, has been described as 'the place where men go to get girls and girls go to get husbands'. This description must originate in its festival in the summer, when dancing, singing, eating, and drinking go on for days, with visitors coming from all over Ireland to join the fun, and from abroad as well. The tide of merriment flows from the town to Doolin beach five miles west and back again. This reputation for high frolics seems to accord little with the image of Lisdoonvara as a sedate spa busying itself with the relief of rheumatism and related maladies, but this too is Lisdoonvara, with sulphur and chalybeate springs still working and highly regarded in a time when spas generally are failing. You may drink the waters or bathe in them.

Lahinch and the Cliffs of Moher

Lahinch was our headquarters for our exploration of this part of Clare. It is a small seaside resort with an arc of yellow sand punctuated by black rocks, among which, when there is a wind, the sea comes in as white breakers. There is a good golf course. The village lies parallel with the sea and has two streets inland on either side of a valley. As we drove in we saw a man carrying a rod and a fine salmon, which he must have caught in the Deelagh river or the Inagh river, which enter the sea north of Lahinch.

To the south there are cliffs, to the north sand dunes and the village of Liscannor, a little place which boasts the birthplace of the inventor of the submarine, John P. Holland. The characteristic west of Ireland form of boat called a currach may be seen at Liscannor, either in operation by fishermen or drawn up by the sea and generally lying upside down like enormous black beetles. The simile is not original. It occurs to everyone who sees these boats for the first time.

West of Liscannor is Liscannor castle, a square keep that belonged to the O Briens. It was an O Brien, Cornelius, who put up the tall Ionic column, topped by a vase, as a memorial to himself, in 1865. It was paid for by subscription by his tenants and there are some who say that the subscribers were not willing. Others say that Cornelius was a benign landlord who did much for his tenants. He was Member of Parliament at Westminster for the county of Clare, and thus a successor of Daniel O Connell.

A road north brings us near to the Cliffs of Moher, five miles of some of the most stupendous cliffs in Ireland. The thing about these cliffs is that they go straight down vertically to the sea without any scree at the foot, and this gives their 700 feet of sheer fall added impressiveness and awe. The cliffs appear to have narrow horizontal white bands, but these turn out to be numbers of seabirds that gather on the cliff faces. There seems to be little for them to cling to.

A round turret-like structure on the highest part of the cliffs was put up by Cornelius O Brien as a kind of belvedere.

The height of the cliffs is a little misleading – they are much higher than you might suppose, and it is not until a cow or a horse is seen grazing on the cliff tops that one really has a criterion. The animal will appear frighteningly small.

Out to sea appear the islands of Aran, grey in the sunlight and indeed of the same kind of limestone as much of Clare and the Burren. Aran is considered part of county Galway, but physically it is part of Clare, with the same kind of geology and many of the same kinds of flowers as make the Burren gay in spring. The islands appear like a fleet of old-fashioned battleships steaming straight for the coast of Clare. The smallest of the three main islands comes first, and this is Inisheer, then follows Inishmaan, and third Inishmore. Last come the little Brannock Islands, but these are no more than a cockleboat in tow in a most un-navylike manner.

The extent of sea between Inisheer and the mainland is known as the South Sound.

The west coast and Loop Head

We drove down southwards in the morning, between Milltown Malbay and Slieve Callan, a mountain by name but no more than 1282 feet high. It carries a bogus ogham stone – not an altogether unheard of thing, but why should anybody want to fake ogham stones? Also on Slieve Callan stands a cromlech or dolmen, which in fact is a passage grave. It is popularly known as Diarmuid and Gráinne's Bed. The story of Diarmuid and Gráinne is an Irish version of the legend of Tristram and Iseult.

Spanish Point, west of Milltown Malbay is so named from the galleons of the fleeing Armada, which sailed from the English Channel through the North Sea and around the coast of Scotland in their attempt to get back to Spain. But they struck here at Spanish Point, and by order of the English governor of Connacht, Bingham, there was a company of men who had followed the ships along the shore and were waiting to dispatch the Spaniards as they landed. The bodies were buried on the point and the golfers of today may play over their unheeding heads.

The road from Milltown Malbay approaches the shore and comes to the curiously named village of Quilty, a name which somehow does not seem Irish. But it is in fact the Irish word 'coillte', which means woods. No matter if woods are few at Quilty now; the name remains. Instead of woods to draw attention there are masses of seaweed, piles of it everywhere, with dark festoons of ribbonweed hanging on walls. You may see more of it being collected where it grows on the seashore. And everywhere there is the clammy, salty odour of seaweed. It was once kept to dry for months and then burned, the ash being used for the production of iodine. This was one of the most common industries in the west of Ireland in the nineteenth century. But the manufacture of iodine was eventually synthesised and carried out in some other way and the fires of burning kelp were extinguished and were no longer seen in the districts by the sea, where once their thick smoke, curling to the sky, had marked an industry. The end of the making of kelp meant hardship for the country people, for many of whom it had helped to stave off famine – but a demand is back, and seaweed is gathered as before, to be used at home as fertiliser on the land, as it always was, or exported for the production of alginates, which go into many foodstuffs and beverages such as bread, jellies of various kinds, and beer and stout, where they produce the creamy head.

You will see that badge of the west, the currach, at Quilty, perhaps at work on the sea or lying upside down and weighted down with large stones lest the strong winds from the sea should blow it away where it stands before the little stone, whitewashed cottages.

In 1907 the men of the village put out one stormy night to rescue the crew of a French ship wrecked off this rocky coast. In gratitude the Frenchmen raised a subscription to pay for a new church for Quilty. The church is there today to remind the visitor of this episode, and a curious little church it is. The architect evidently determined that in this place of the far west the church ought to be visibly Celtic, and its grey stone walls and steep roof recall the style of the early churches of the saints. It even boasts a 'round tower' springing from the roof, but not as big as the towers that defied the Vikings.

Kilkee is a very pretty seaside resort in miniature, at the head of Moore Bay and at the root of the Loop Head peninsula. There are several hotels and guest-houses. The bay is deep between headlands, with a wide, smooth stretch of sand, across which runs a shallow stream to the sea. The little town is modern, but not too up-to-date for ass-carts to be seen in the streets.

The Catholic church of St. Senan evidently owes something of its design to Coventry cathedral. There is the same arrangement of long and narrow windows facing the altar, with beautiful stained glass; but it should be added that the design perhaps owes as much to the church of Christ the King in Cork, which antedates Coventry by many years.

There are excellent walks over the cliffs. West of the bay are the Duggerna Rocks, where the road from the beach climbs above a great apron of rock in which there are natural bathing pools. But bathers should beware. The rocks are of a laminated strata, and it is possible to clamber round the edge of a pool supposing yourself in only a few feet of water, when suddenly you step over the edge of a shelf and fall into a depth. One of these pools, the Newfoundout, has springboards for diving.

A path leads across the cliff tops to a large hollow in the horizontal strata, where this structure of laminated shelves may be seen. This hollow, sometimes called the Amphitheatre, is occasionally used for concerts. Continue on the path and you come to a puffing-hole, where the sea has tunnelled out a cave and burst its roof. There are several caves at Kilkee.

Loop Head is the tongue of land extending westwards between, on the south, the Shannon estuary and on the north the Atlantic. The headland has much interesting and impressive cliff scenery, with little islands or stacks broken off from the peninsula and separated by heaving seas. Bishop's Island, near Fooagh, is one such with a flat grassy top on which, and inaccessible, are scanty remains of St. Senan's oratory. Intrinsic Bay is named after a ship, the *Intrinsic*, wrecked here in 1836.

A sailing-ship, blown on shore, had little chance on this coast. Strong winds are characteristic of Loop Head, as you may deduce from the fact that the thatch of the cottage roofs is held down by a network of cords pegged to the stone walls.

Take time off your sea-and-landscape-gazing to visit the little modern church of the village of Cross, to see the kind of forward thinking applied to Catholic village churches these days. The pleasant stained glass of the paired lancet windows depicts the stations of the Cross and the mysteries of the Rosary, subjects more often encountered elsewhere as very mediocre Victorian paintings or even worse conventional sculptures.

The bridges of Ross are natural rock arches near the end of the peninsula. A short walk will bring them in sight, standing close together with the sea heaving through the apertures it has created by beating against the curved strata. The bridges are part of an impressive cliff-scape that is in every sense worth the walk, even if phenomena such as the bridges leaves you uninterested. There were two bridges when I last saw them. One of them looked very battered and as though a few more storms and beatings by the sea might knock it down.

Moneen is an undistinguished and scattered village above the sea, memorable only for its possession of the Little Ark. This is a plain, caravan-like structure kept in the church. It came about as a substitute. When the parishioners wanted to build a Catholic church, the landowners, who were all Protestant, would not allow land for it. So the Little Ark was built. At mass time, when that co-incided with low tide, the Ark was hauled down below high water level to shelter the priest and the altar. The congregation stood on the beach.

This demonstration, that the parishioners were determined to attend mass in the place of their choosing and out of reach of their objectors, apparently resulted eventually, after much bitterness, in the building of the present church.

Diarmuid and Gráinne's Rock, near the point of the long peninsula, is yet another of the many rocks or dolmens connected with the legend of the flight of this pair of lovers throughout Ireland, pursued by a vengeful king. But it has another legend, telling of the mighty warrior Cuchulainn and how he fled from a woman. She was called Mal and perhaps he fled from her amorous pursuit because she was a witch. She followed him along the cliffs until they came opposite Diarmuid and Gráinne's rock, which is an isolated stack with a channel of the sea separating it from the mainland. Cuchulainn, seeing that Mal was still coming, took a running jump and cleared the intervening channel of water to land on the top of the rock. There, no doubt, he thought himself safe, and perhaps he was about to thumb his nose at Mal when she took a great leap and landed beside him. If Cuchulainn jumped with surprise at this feat it might be the truth, for the start it gave him took him back to the mainland! Poor Mal, however, could not manage this return journey and she fell into the sea and was drowned. She bled so copiously, as witches do, that her blood stained the sea far to the north, and that is how Mal Bay came to get its name.

Loop Head is a long, narrow tongue of land raised for the most part a couple of hundred feet above the sea and bordered by steep cliffs. It has little surface relief and the cottages in the winter have no shelter from the terrific winds that blow from across the Atlantic.

A lighthouse rises at the extreme western point of Loop Head, but I do not think that it is open to the public without special arrangements with Dublin. Probably, as is the case with many Irish lighthouses, it is now automatic.

The road signs lead the way to Carrigaholt, a small village with a college of Irish, where students of the language come to acquire the *blas* – that is, a good Irish accent. Down by the sea stands the slender tower-house of Carrigaholt, complete in its bawn; it has a lively story. Though it could never have been more than a cramped habitation, a number of people desired it and some were willing to fight for it. It was built by the Mac Mahon lords of Corcabascin in the late fifteenth century, and one of these was besieged in the tower in 1598, unsuccessfully, by Sir Conyers Clifford. Shortly after Clifford gave up the siege as a bad job, the tower was captured by the Earl of Thomond. The tower then fell into the capacious hands of the O Briens, who built the fireplace on the fifth floor – the principal chamber – and dated it 1603. The tower was taken in 1651 and it was overcome by the Cromwellian General Ludlow and held for a year. In 1666 Charles II gave it back to the O Briens. Forty years later William of Orange gave it to Keppel, Earl of Albemarle, who sold it at once to a family called Burton, who held it then for some 250 years. Carrigaholt is an interesting study as a defensive tower-house, with its musket loops. The holes in the roof of the entrance tunnel were called 'murder holes' and were meant to enable the defenders to drop things on the heads of intruders. The bawn too, the wall around the courtyard of the castle, is an unusual survival.

Originally the tower would have been much darker and grimmer inside than it is now. Many of the windows are sixteenth-century insertions.

The tower saw the raising of Clare's dragoons, an expatriate force famous in Irish history, which fought for the French in the war against England. Lord Clare, an O Brien, was responsible for its creation after the defeat of King James at the Boyne; he drilled his dragoons in the field next to the castle.

From Carrigaholt we follow the road to Kilrush, at a little distance from but with glimpses of that great sheet of water that one is always surprised to discover is still the Shannon. Kilrush, though not a large place, is the second largest town in the county of Clare. It has a wide street of colour-washed Georgian houses leading to the sea and Kilrush's port of Cappagh. The church of Kilrush was built in the nineteenth century by a designer who seems to have confused a church with a castle and thought battlements were called for. It is worth visiting for the sake of some fine Harry Clarke windows.

From the stone pier of Kilrush you may look out over the low-lying Hog Island to Scattery Island, which you may visit if you will take the trouble to inquire for a boatman – Scattery lies about two miles from Cappagh. The island takes its name from a saint called Cathaigh – Inis Cathaigh, Cathaigh's island, gives us 'Scattery' – but the saint more closely associated with it is St. Senan, who flourished in the sixth century. He founded a monastery on the island, and for some time this flourished. But an island in the broad Shannon was too convenient and too tempting a place for the acquisitive and aggressive Norse sea rovers and they raided the island several times. There remain ruins of five churches and of a round tower, and a great reputation for holiness which has persisted for fourteen hundred years. Such was the confidence of the monks in their security on the island that though they built a round tower and made it very tall – 115 feet – they set the door at ground level instead of putting it twelve or fifteen feet up.

The building called the 'cathedral' is a single chamber being 68 feet by 27½ feet dating from the ninth or tenth century, with pointed windows inserted three or four hundred years later. The other churches – the oratory, Teampall Senan, and Teampall na Marbh (Church of the Dead) – are mostly medieval with restorations. St. Senan is said to be buried in St. Senan's Bed, a walled enclosure near Teampall Senan. Among the gravestones are two early slabs and an incised cross with the inscriptions 'Ór do Móinach' and 'Ór do Mónach aite Mógroin', 'Pray for Mónach' and 'Pray for Mónach, tutor of Mógron'.

There is nothing to distinguish Killimer on the mainland but the memory of Ellen Hanly, and her only claim to renown is that her husband chose to murder her one day in July 1819. Gerald Griffin used the murder of Ellen Hanly in his novel *The Collegians*, which in turn inspired Dion Boucicault's play *The Colleen Bawn*, and from this was derived the opera *The Lily of Killarney* by Benedict, who changed the locale to Killarney. The schoolmaster of Kilrush provided a grave and a tombstone for Ellen Hanly, but the stone was chipped away by dolts in search of souvenirs and nothing remains of it. Poor Ellen Hanly! Her murder seems to have acquired the lasting notoriety that is reserved for some quite unremarkable crimes, as, for instance, the murder of Maria Martin in the Red Barn.

The Burren

The Burren is a tract of country that includes a large part of northern county Clare, and might also be said to include the Aran Islands. As we have seen, there is an information centre about the Burren at Kilfenora. The distinction of the Burren lies basically in its geological formation. It is mostly composed of limestone terraces and clints, with some shale, and the effect is an astounding wilderness of a kind of country called '*karst*' after a similar terrain in central Europe – a nearer comparison would be the limestone country above Malham in Yorkshire.

The Burren is remarkable for its flowers. The climate is mild and damp and favours the growth of many plants that are familiar farther south on the Mediterranean littoral and in the Alpine regions as well as those normally to be found in this part of Ireland, and the result is a flora of astonishing richness, all the more surprising that it has to discover root in niches and cracks among the limestone. Botanists find much to delight and interest them in the Burren.

Speleologists also find much to interest them, including the longest cave in Ireland, Pollnagollum, on the eastern slopes of Mount Elva. It is seven miles long, as far as exploration has gone. Limestone country is typically full of holes and disappearing streams, and in the Burren, of transient lakes, called 'turlochs', which exist on the surface in the winter but dry up or drain away in the summer, leaving a green hollow.

Archæologists, further, are fascinated by the Burren, with the evidence of a number of dolmens pointing to the presence of a prehistoric population.

The local Irish farmers find in this wilderness water enough, and sufficient grazing among the stones and terraces, but the Burren certainly has the appearance of a dry and stony wilderness. It makes interesting walking country, strange and often spectacular, and there are several roads along which it may be penetrated by car. These include Kilfenora to Lisdoonvara and on to Ballyvaghan, and the Corkscrew Road, so-called from its twists and turns, from Ballyvaghan to Corofin.

2
South County Galway

Coming from Dublin, with your face to the west, you pass over the great central plain of Ireland, through Kildare and West Meath, sometimes through good farming country, well treed and comfortable, sometimes through bogland sad and dark, to cross Ireland's largest river, the Shannon, at Athlone – an ancient crossing place, for the name means a ford: *Áth Luain*, the ford of the meadow. Beyond Athlone you are in a different county and in a different province – in the county of Galway in Connacht. The shining Shannon is the division between provinces, flowing down from the north through the complexities and the islands of Loch Ree as a hidden current, before it again becomes plainly a river, passing beneath the bridge of Athlone, where King William's men fought the Irish in 1691 and won. Far to the South the Shannon becomes a current once more, through the beautiful lake of Loch Derg, through which it goes to Killaloe and Limerick.

Ballinasloe to Loughrea

A good, if sinuous, road goes from Athlone to Ballinasloe, a town beside the river Suck, centring on a square overlooked by a grey granite gothic church of 1858 designed by Pugin and Mac Carthy, designers of the silvery cathedral of Killarney. Ballinasloe is a quiet agricultural town until October comes along, and then it lets its hair down and its enthusiasm spills over in a great and varied fair. The town could once boast of the largest horse-fair in Europe, and if this superlative is no longer applicable, large numbers of horses are still put up for sale on a Sunday on the fair green, and there are horse-jumping competitions as well. The fair and the festival go on for a week.

Eight miles to the west the lovely Franciscan friary of Kilconnell rises beyond the houses of the small village. It was founded in 1353 by William O Kelly and reconstructed in 1414, it later became Observantine, the 'observation' referring to poverty and economy, to which the order was vowed. In 1596 an English garrison occupied the friary and 57 years later Cromwellians besieged it, without success. The friary is now a ruin, but the church and some of the claustral buildings stand to the eaves. The general plan is common among Franciscan friaries, with a long nave and chancel to the church, joining beneath a tall and slender central tower that belongs to the later rebuilding, and there is a cloister with pointed arches. Near the small but charming west door of the church is a fine tomb with flamboyant tracery that would be considered fourteenth-century in England and is much later in Ireland; it shows along the tomb-chest six figures of saints, with their names, homely and attractive people. Under the tower the angel corbels are accompanied by a little carving of an owl in high relief – an expression of *joie de vivre* of the sculptor perhaps; but it may be that a carved owl helped to frighten small birds and bats out of the church.

In the guardian's lodging Matthew Barnewell, 12th Lord Trimleston, has a stone with lettering flowing round his coat of arms; it says that he was 'transplanted' into Connacht by 'the usurper Cromwell', an effect of the Cromwellian resolve to drive the Irish 'to hell or Connacht'. Even a man with a name as English as Barnewell was not exempt: no doubt he was a Catholic landowner and that was enough.

South-east of Kilconnell at Aughrim in July 1691 the Irish army commanded by the French general St. Ruth made a stand on Kilcommadaun Hill after being driven out of Athlone. The opposing commander was Ginkel. St. Ruth appears to have been a singularly incompetent soldier, as well as a vainglorious one. At Aughrim, however, he was killed by a cannon-ball and the Irish retreated to Limerick, to be besieged there by King William.

Here in the Shannon valley there is a lush and peaceful landscape, ornamented by trees and hedges and fields of green grass. It repaid the labour of the many monks and friars who worked it, as at Kilconnell and Clontuskert. The element 'clon' in the latter name means a meadow. The abbey of Clontuskert was one of the most prosperous in this district, with a long history, for it was founded by St. Baodan in the ninth century. The monks rebuilt it in the thirteenth and fourteenth centuries, and rebuilt it again after it was burned down in 1413, although there were then only the prior and 12 canons. The money for the work came from the sale of 10-year indulgences. As in many other instances in Ireland, the monks ignored the Reformation, carrying on as before in monasteries nominally dissolved. But Cromwell was more positive in this matter, and he left the buildings a sorry wreck. There are some interesting carved details, including a pretty west doorway of 1471, with a pelican vulning and a mermaid admiring herself in a mirror – mermaids are not uncommon in ecclesiastical art.

A few miles to the south-west at Clonfert St. Brendan, called the Navigator, founded a monastery in the year 558. He is said to have been buried here, as he is also said to have died at Annaghdown, another of his foundations. St. Brendan was 'the Navigator' because, according to persistent tradition, he sailed across the western seas and discovered America, inspired by a vision of distant lands he had seen from the summit of Mount Brendan in Kerry. His vessel could only have been a large currach of lath and leather and such a voyage must have been a dire experience; yet it may well be the truth that he visited Iceland, Greenland, Newfoundland, and Labrador nearly a thousand years before Columbus. In 1976 a brave adventurer emulated this voyage by sailing in a leather currach to Newfoundland, proving at least that Brendan's voyage was possible.

The earliest part of the present church of Clonfert (which is still called a cathedral) dates from the twelfth century. It is an astonishing romanesque west doorway, of barbaric splendour, and all the more amazing for the minuscule size of the church to which it is the entrance. The seven orders of the doorway have inclined jambs – an Irish custom of the time (an eighth order of whiter stone inserted in the fifteenth century has vertical sides). Above them, within a tall, steep-sided triangular hood-mould, rows of primitively carved heads gaze down on the visitor. Inside the little church there are several things worth seeing – a fifteenth-century font, some seventeenth-century monuments, and ancient gravestones with a plea for a prayer – 'Ór do Baclat', pray for Baclat, for example. Among the interesting carvings on the thirteenth-century east window is another mermaid.

The ruined house behind the cathedral of Clonfert was the bishop's palace; it was burned down in 1950, when it was owned by Sir Oswald Mosley. The see of Clonfert is now centred at Loughrea.

From Clonfert we go south-west, still in the Shannon valley, to Eyrecourt, a small village ending in a square; here the novelist Charles Lever found the original of his eponymous hero Charles O Malley in George Eyre, of the family that gave the village its name. Two fanciful gateways lead into the demesne in which their house once stood. Not very exciting country, but we are venturing into this quiet and peaceful corner of county Galway in order to visit two castles that are excellent examples of the many tower-houses the remains of which are found all over Ireland, dating from the fifteenth, sixteenth, and seventeenth centuries.

Tower-houses, as I have said, were the homes of the landowners and chiefs of the time, homes that of necessity had to be fortified against attack by the English and against other Irish chiefs who might have had their eye on the possibility of the agrandissement of their property at the expense of their neighbours. The tower, strongly built of stone, as you may see, generally comprised three to five floors one above the other, in many instances with one of the upper floors supported on a vault. The vault was built of stones and mortar on a centring of woven hurdles or wattles, and if you look for it the impress of the wattles on the underside of the vault may be seen. It was not a true arch, for there was no keystone, but tower and vault formed one structure of extraordinary strength that could not easily be made to collapse. That is one reason why so many tower-houses still stand in the Irish landscape. The floors were connected by stone spiral stairs, when there was room, but some tower-houses were quite small in area, and then, it seems, there must have been a wooden stair or even a ladder. The principal chamber of a tower-house was usually one down from the top with the bed-chambers above that. Here on these two floors the owner and his family lived in what we should consider a high degree of discomfort and uncertainty.

Their one connection with the exterior, and the route by which all goods and services had to come – food, water, fuel, servants, and men at arms – was by the narrow stone vice, spiralling round the central newel. But if it had disadvantages, the stair also had an advantage: it confined attackers to a narrow route and thus was easy to defend. And if the vice was clockwise, as it frequently was, it was deliberately so, for this gave the defender freedom for his right arm and equally kept the attacker at a disadvantage against the newel and the narrow part of the wedge of the stair.

On one of the upper floors some tower-houses had a concealed recess which was in effect the safe hiding-place for the owner's valuables and money. Sometimes this recess was approached through a garderobe in the thickness of the wall – the term 'garderobe' is not medieval, but the middle ages no more than we had no satisfactory term for what we call 'the smallest room', 'toilet', or 'loo'. In a tower-house, as in medieval castles generally, this necessary feature was hidden in the wall, in many instances approached by a dark corridor with one or two right-angled turns. It vented straight down the wall on to the ground or into a ditch, and this part of the structure must have been very nasty.

A tower-house had guard-rooms and store-rooms on the lower floors, and on the ground-floor was commonly a recess by the entrance, for a porter. A visitor would have to pass him, and would also have to pass beneath a 'murder-hole' – a hole in the roof of the entrance passage through which, if he were not welcome, unpleasant things like boiling oil and molten lead could be dropped on him.

A tower-house had an additional defence that may not now be visible. This was a surrounding wall, known as a 'bawn'. The bawn has more often than not disappeared or survives only in part.

Derryhiveney castle, three miles north-east of Portumna, is a late example of a tower-house, built in 1643 by Dónal O Madden – his initials and the date are inscribed on a corbel. Dónal O Madden built a substantial and handsome tower standing in an L-shaped bawn, with rounded turrets at diagonally opposite corners. As usual, the lower two of the four storeys were defensive, with few and utilitarian openings. In the third and fourth storeys the windows are in pairs divided by mullions. Above these, on the eaves line, corbelled machicolations jut out from diagonally opposite corners – it is a surprising fact that tower-house builders considered that defence by machicolations or bartizans was required only on two angles.

You may look up the wedge-shaped steps around the newel from floor to floor and imagine the manner of life of the O Maddens in their restricted quarters, with everything – all the traffic of the household and its garrison – passing up and down those awkward and perilous stone steps. The inhabitants kept themselves warm by burning logs and faggots in the spacious fireplaces, the chimneys of which give a distinctive outline to the ruin.

Three miles to the south the little town of Portumna stands at the head of the large and intricate Loch Derg, a very beautiful lake whose cerulean waters are well seen from the slopes of the Slieve Auchty mountains. Never mind that the Slieve Auchtys do not exceed 1207 feet in their highest summit, Cashlaundrumlahan – the music of that name and the views of sea and lake the Slieve Auchtys confer are enough to excuse the exaggeration of the term 'mountain'.

Portumna is a small town emphasised by the striking detached tower of its modern Catholic church. It is a boating and angling centre, with salmon, trout, perch, rudd, pike, bream, and tench waiting to give the fisherman a run for his bait. The afforested demesne of Portumna castle contains the remains of a fine house (not a tower-house) built in the seventeenth century, probably by the Burkes, and later the property of the earls and marquesses of Clanrickarde. It survived sieges by the Cromwellians in 1659 and by the Williamites in 1690, to be accidentally burned out in 1826. A stone set in the crumbling walls by the double staircase is an affecting and sentimental tablet to a dog that died in April 1797 – '. . . Alas poor Fury, she was a dog taken all in all I shall not look upon her like again'.

A Dominican friary near the castle was founded in 1426 by an O Madden and was destroyed by Cromwellians in 1641. It has beautiful windows in the east and south transepts, and there are a number of seventeenth-century memorial tablets with relief lettering of a style that you will encounter again in many places in the west.

About six miles from Portumna along the Loughrea road stands the second of the two tower-houses I would like you to see. Pallas castle is a ruin, but it is a ruin evocative of a tower-house in its heyday, with its bawn practically complete and larger than most. Built in the sixteenth century by the Burkes, the tower demonstrates by its narrow windows even on the upper floors the dangers of its day and the over-powering need for defence – only on the fourth floor was it deemed safe to allow mullioned windows big enough to admit adequate light and air. The bawn is practically complete, with a two-storey gatehouse and the 'allure' or wall-walk along which the defenders kept guard. By the seventeenth century the castle was in the hands of the Nugents, who built a more comfortable dwelling projecting into the bawn near the tower. Of this house only a chimneyed gable remains, pierced by mullioned windows.

To the north at Tynagh lead and zinc are mined, a rare instance of heavy industry in the west of Ireland.

With its colour-washed houses along its main street pleasantly sited on the northern shore of the loch from which it takes its name, Loughrea is the cathedral town of the Catholic diocese of Clonfert. In ancient times the lake was the site of a number of crannógs, the artificial islands constructed of logs and brushwood to carry dwellings, mere huts or shacks, isolated from the dangers of the shore. In the middle ages

Loughrea was a walled town, the principal seat of those descendants of the Norman de Burgos, the Mac William Uachtar Burkes, who held the title of Earls of Clanrickarde. All that remains of the fortifications is the fifteenth-century town gate-house, near the cathedral; the gate-house is now a museum of ecclesiastical art for the diocese of Clonfert.

The cathedral of St. Brendan was built between 1897 and 1903 to the design of the architect William Byrne, to succeed the little church of St. Brendan that we have seen at Clonfert. Byrne's cathedral, though massive in impression and crowned by a spire, is not really very large as cathedrals go, nor especially interesting outside; but it is well worth inspecting for its interior decoration and furnishing – for the colourful windows of stained glass by Sarah Purser and other members of her Tower of Glass (a conspectus of the best glass of the time – with the exception of Harry Clarke); and for stations of the Cross by Ethel Rhind, a statue of the Virgin and Child by John Hughes, embroidered sodality banners by Jack B Yeats, the remarkable artist brother of the poet, altar rails and ironwork by Michael Scott, and much more. Though still entitled to the term 'modern' these things are now sufficiently of the past to be regarded dispassionately, but not too dispassionately for admiration.

Beyond the cathedral the grey-blue waters of the lake stretch to the misty planes of the Slieve Auchtys.

The castle in which the Mac William Uachter Burkes dwelt at Loughrea has gone, but there are remains, distinctly overrestored, of the Carmelite friary founded in 1300 by Richard de Burgo. It stands near the modern buildings of a priory of Discalced Carmelites. These friars wear a brown habit, not the white you might expect of Carmelites, who were of course known as Whitefriars. 'Discalced' means 'shoeless' – a young friar I spoke with was wearing sandals.

The Turoe stone to Coole

Four miles north of the town, signposted from the hamlet of Bullaun, there is a remarkable curiosity, the Turoe stone. It is a boulder, apparently artificially rounded, by a circular iron cattlegrid that prevents cattle using it as a rubbing-post – although on its previous site beside a now-demolished earthwork fort it may have assuaged the itch of bovine hides through two thousand years and more. The stone, about three-feet high, bears a sculptured low-relief design of considerable interest. The lower part is plain. Then comes a simple key pattern that seems to suggest a connection, however distant, with Greece. The upper part bears a swirling mass of opposed spirals, which were achieved by cutting away the background to leave the pattern in relief. The magic of the spiral, the movement of the whorled line of the La Tène phase of iron-age Celtic art, enchanted artists and designers for centuries. It passed from incised stone to beaten or engraved metal, and so to the richly coloured pages of illuminated manuscripts, in which the spiral, speaking once of a pagan ethic, was brought within the expression of Christian thought, continuing, as it had for so many centuries, to serve a need of the Celtic imagination. You may, if you wish, regard the Turoe stone simply as an art object, an abstract design satisfying for itself and needing no explanation; but it is unlikely that it was made for mere self-expression, any more than were the spirally engraved boulder at Castlestrange in Roscommon and the stones of the burial chamber at Newgrange. The Turoe Stone shows a more complex, more subtly sculpted pattern than these; yet it surely must have served also a ritual purpose.

About ten miles south-west of Loughrea Edward Martyn lived at Tullira castle, a neo-gothic structure of 1882. Martyn took a deep interest in Irish art and literature, and he was concerned not only in the foundation of the Abbey Theatre in Dublin, with W. B. Yeats and Lady Gregory, but also in the development of the modern school of Irish stained-glass design, of which the windows of Loughrea cathedral are such interesting examples. Martyn initiated this movement by having a window designed by Christopher Whall for the little church of Laban near Tullira, and through Whall, Martyn brought A. E. Child to Ireland to teach the process. Persuaded by Martyn, Sarah Purser founded the firm of An Túr Gloine (the Tower of Glass), from which henceforth much of the development of the art of stained glass in Ireland flowed.

Edward Martyn was among the remarkable group of people who from time to time were guests of Lady Augusta Gregory at Coole south of Tullira castle. The Gregorys came to Coole in 1768 and lived there in a simple Georgian house of modest size. Here Lady Gregory found deep satisfaction in the books that lined the walls, and added to them many more volumes given to her by writers who were her friends and frequently her guests. They were not always famous – Lady Gregory was quick to appreciate nascent genius. In 1898 W. B. Yeats, then ill and homeless and little known, was brought to Coole and given a room to work in and the freedom of the great demesne, with its walks and woods and lakes. Almost anyone who was or became eminent in Irish literature or art visited Coole, including John Millington Synge, George Bernard Shaw, Seán O Casey, Frank O Connor, and many others who were not Irish. Lady Gregory's 'visitors' book' was a copper beech in the garden, in the bark of which she invited her guests to carve their initials. The passing years have blurred the initials now, but those of W. B. Yeats may be made out, together with those of A. E. (George Russell), Jack B. Yeats, Seán O Casey, and boldest of them all GBS linked in a chain one above the other. Augustus John cut his initials on the bole and climbed the tree to cut them again higher up.

Lady Gregory describes the house room by room, with its contents and many associations, in her book *Coole*, beautifully produced in a limited edition by the Dolmen Press. It was an ideal house for a writer, and here she wrote several plays and short stories in a peasant idiom that are not shamed by the august literary company they keep.

Lady Gregory died aged 80 in 1932. The house passed to the government, who, with astonishing stupidity, sold the building to a contractor, who demolished it for the value of the stone. The footings have been filled in as a kind of grassy plinth that gives the least idea of what Coole was like. The demesne has been taken over by the Forestry Service, which has planted many kinds of useful trees, masking Yeats's Seven Woods of Coole. Signposts point the way to the lake where Yeats saw nine-and-fifty swans and wrote a poem about them. The autograph tree, the widespreading copper beech, is still there, in a walled garden. It is surrounded by high iron railings that deny access to initial-scribing nonentities – Lady Gregory once had to drive off a crowd of American youths who were intent on joining their initials to those of the famous – though, as she said, one of them might have been a future president.

After his first visit in 1892 Yeats came to Coole nearly every year for twenty years. In 1916 he bought a ruined towerhouse for £35 from the Congested Districts Board – it had once belonged to the Gregorys and was only about three and a half miles from Coole. Standing beside the shallow Cloon river, which disappears into the ground a little downstream, the tower was once known as Islandmore castle and had been a property of the de Burgos. Yeats called it Thoor Ballylee. He restored the fabric and lived here until 1920 with his wife George. He set a tablet in the wall dedicating the tower to her in a short verse that foresaw the future ruin of the building, and indeed the tower did become a ruin once more, with frightening rapidity, after the Yeats's ceased to come here. It was restored once more, by Bord Fáilte, and was opened in 1965, the centenary of the birth of W. B. Yeats, as a Yeats memorial. It contains some of the furniture he used and a collection of Yeatsiana (*Plate* 1).

Gort and disappearing rivers

Southwards by the Tll is the town of Gort, a pleasant little market-town with flowering trees in its streets and a statue of Christ overlooking the market-place. The market in an Irish provincial town was always picturesque, bustling, and noisy as goods and cattle were brought in for sale and weights were checked in the weigh-house. Because of the cattle and the many horses the air was generally odorous and the streets soggy with ordure. Nowadays markets are not what they were, beasts are kept out of the streets, and sales are held at auction marts out of the town. In the square I found the weigh-house with its windows smashed and its machinery rusty. A tradition has died, says a tourist regretfully. 'And a good job too', retorts the pratical town-dweller.

'Gort' means a field – *Gort Inse Guaire*, the holm field of Guaire. The seventh-century king Guaire had a castle or palace at Kinvara, by the sea north-west of Gort. There he entertained with such generosity that his right arm, his 'giving arm', was said to have become longer than his left. Perhaps he did not feel quite so generous when, as he sat down to eat his supper one day, all the dishes rose and flew out of the window. They sailed across the fields to alight before St. Colman, who had, providentially, at that moment concluded a seven-year fast. But the wrathful king, who had followed on horeseback, found that the saint was a distant relative, so that was all right. The king gave Colman land at Kilmacduagh, where the saint founded a monastery, the ruins of which are still to be seen.

St. Colman's monastery of Kilmacduagh – Duagh was Colman's father – will be found south-west of Gort near the county boundary. Though little of it, it seems, can belong to Colman's time, the seventh century, the present buildings, going back as far as the tenth century, form one of the most interesting groups of ecclesiastical structures in Ireland. There are remains of five churches, monastic buildings, a round tower, and a fortified house.

The most important building of the complex is the monastic church of Templemore Mac Duagh, which became the cathedral of a diocese in the twelfth century. It has a short nave of the tenth or eleventh century, crossing of the twelfth, and transepts and a chancel of the fifteenth. Roofless now, it remains to eaves height. In the north transept is a huge tomb-chest of the O Shaughnessys, with above it a low-relief of the Crucifixion in a lettered frame, probably seventeenth century. Next to this is another relief, of St. Colman, with bishop's mitre and huge crozier. A second Crucifixion carving is to be seen on a monument on the north wall. On a jamb of the door is an incised comic face with ear-rings.

The round tower, near the cathedral and a small lake, was built in the eleventh or twelfth century, and is a very fine example, 112 feet high. That it was intended to serve as a refuge in time of attack is shown by the fact that the door is 26 feet from the ground; it no doubt served also as a belfry – the Irish word for a round tower, *cloigtheach*, in fact means a belfry. The monks taking refuge in the tower, with their treasures, would be safe from any hit-and-grab invader, once the ladder by which they had entered was drawn up; they would not be so secure from anyone who had time to smoke them out – a round tower could have made an effective flue. Near the tower is the grave of Bishop French, who died in 1852; he lies reputedly on the site of the grave of St. Colman.

The tower leans slightly out of the vertical. If you fear that it will fall you may comfort yourself with the thought that it has probably been like that for the better part of a millennium.

Teampall Mhuire, St. Mary's church, east of the cathedral on the other side of the road that runs through the site, is a small, thirteenth-century building lighted by only two narrow lancet windows. O Hyne's monastery, or the abbey church, north-west of the cathedral, is an impressive twelfth-to thirteenth-century church with good windows and carving. Attached to it is a monastic building adapted as a mausoleum. The Abbot's House, beyond a lane, is a fortified fourteenth- or fifteenth-century rectangular building with gun-loops on the ground floor and twin trefoiled lancets above. The remaining two churches are small and their masonry residual.

The site is now a quiet field sloping away from the road and the round tower. It must once have been busy with human activity as the monks followed their routine of prayer, devotion, and labour, always under the threat of interruption from the Norse or from dissensions of the native rulers.

West of Kilmacduagh lies Loch Cutra, an irregular lake, with the demesne of Loch Cutra castle on its south-west shore. The castle, a handsome neo-gothic building, was put up in 1810 by the brothers George and Richard Pain to the design of John Nash, for Lord Gort. It was sold several times and was twice re-bought by succeeding Lords

Gort. The latest of the Gort owners, Viscount Gort, began an intensive restoration and this was continued by a new owner in 1971. The castle has been open to the public for some years.

We saw that the river flowing at the foot of Yeats's Thoor Ballylee disappeared into the ground. This is only one of a number of curious appearances and disappearances of rivers in this limestone district. The ground must be honeycombed with water-filled halls and caverns. Occasionally rivers rise to the daylight and promptly disappear again, as at the Punchbowl about a mile south of Gort. The Punchbowl is a huge, funnel-shaped hollow, surrounded by trees, with water swirling sullenly at the bottom, a dangerous place and an impressive one. Not far away, near the Limerick road, another river comes out of a cliff face, flows for a short distance, and vanishes into the Blackwater Hole. At Cannahowna, a mile to the east of the Punchbowl, the road runs over a natural bridge, below which the Cannahowna river flows from a great arched tunnel, which extends a mile underground. There are several other examples of these striking phenomena within a few miles. The Punchbowl, which is only a few yards from a road, is one of the most convenient for the tourist to see.

Kinvara to Owenmore

At Kinvara in the fifteenth century Rory More O Shaughnessy built a successor to Guaire's castle, and this castle, beautifully sited on a little jutting promontory beside the bay, still stands, a tower-house within the strong walls of its close-fitting bawn. It has been restored, and medieval banquets are held here on summer evenings. Guests, served by girls in colourful costume in a bijou 'great' hall, may listen to readings of Irish literature – the justification for a literary evening rests on the fact that the castle was owned briefly by the writer Dr. St. John Gogarty – while you eat your meal and drink your 'sangria' with some assurance that the dishes, unlike those of King Guaire, will remain on the table.

To the north the castle looks over the waters of Galway Bay to the hills of Iar-Chonnacht and the mountains of Connemara. The windows to the south frame the grey and hazy hills of the Burren in county Clare. The Burren is the curious country in which limestone lies as barren terraces rising to 1109 feet on Slieve Elva. It looks from a distance like country in which no-one could make a living, and so it was reported to Cromwell, a report that was no doubt influential in persuading that amiable gentleman that the west was where he ought to send the Irish.

Yet people have lived in the Burren since prehistoric times, farming the meagre soil, and, dying, have left their monuments as numerous megaliths, grey stone balanced on grey stone. As these men roamed the hills in those far springs and summers they must have admired the amazing flora that flourished in the fissures and hollows.

The road from Kinvara goes past the head of the peninsula on which is Duras House, once the home of a French *émigré*, Count Florimund de Basterot, who brought here such French notables as Maupassant and Maurice Barrès and also entertained Yeats and other founders of the Irish literary renaissance of the turn of the century – indeed it was here, according to Yeats, that the first ideas for national theatre, which became the Abbey, were discussed between Yeats, Lady Gregory, and Edward Martyn.

At 'Burren Pier' near Newquay Bernard Shaw placed part IV of *Man and Superman*, 'The Tragedy of an Elderly Gentleman'. Shaw speaks of hills topped with granite, but there is no granite here. There is nothing but limestone wherever you look, unless you turn your eyes northwards and look across Galway Bay to the distant hills of Iar-Chonnacht.

In a green and fertile valley in the twelfth century an O Brien King of Thomond founded the Franciscan friary of Corcomroe. The monastic buildings have almost completely vanished, but the church remains, set in a cemetery among fields. It is worth a visit for the carving of capitals and other details, including an effigy of Conor na Siudine O Brien, who died in 1267 and looks vaguely as though he might be smoking a pipe.

Northwards from Kinvara the T69 runs inland with little sideroads turning west to the islanded waters of the inner reaches of Galway Bay. One of these roads leads to the ancient monastic site of Drumacoo, which was dedicated to a nun, St. Sourney or Assournaidhe. She lived in the sixth century, and it may be that the lintelled doorway and the massive masonry of the south-western part of the church that still stands here go back nearly to her time. In the thirteenth century, perhaps when the hospitable Abbot Fachtna O Halgaith kept open house for passing scholars – surely never numerous – the church was extended, with an ornate south doorway, unexpectedly sophisticated and up to date so far distant from the developing gothic fashions of France and England; it is a very beautiful doorway. The church was extended again in 1830, in a dull, utilitarian style, apparently to receive the graves and tombstones of the local gentry, whose roofless 'big house of Tyrone' mav be seen across the fields and a maze of walls.

The churchyard is so full of ankle-cracking slabs tilted at all angles that the existence of St. Sourney's well may escape you. The well is outside the churchyard wall, a circle of dry stone with a weedy pool of water in the middle of it.

You may see on the little piers or in the shallow water along the shores of Galway Bay evidence of an extensive oyster fishery. There is a great oyster festival in September, when Paddy Burke's premises at Clarinbridge resound to many accents and tongues. Celebration erupts in all the hamlets between here and Galway town.

At Oranmore a large tower-house beside the sea is complete and inhabited, restored by the writer Anita Leslie and her husband. The lane to it comes to an end facing the castle, but you may clamber along the quay to reach the stony beach beyond. Oranmore may be compared with Thoor Ballylee, both castles restored by literary people in search of peace and quiet.

From Oranmore the road goes sedately into Galway town.

3
Loch Corrib and East County Galway

Among the pleasures and the ornaments of the west of Ireland are its many lakes, which reflect with a deep intensity the cerulean skies of a summer's day. The lakes vary in extent from little shreds of colour scattered among bogs and stones to great expanses on which the wind can whip up white horses under thunderous skies. North of Galway three of the largest lakes of Ireland lie like a barrier against the mountains of the west – against Iar-Connacht, Joyce's Country, and Connemara, and the mountains of the Maumturks, the Partrys, and the Twelve Bens.

Loch Corrib to Tuam

Loch Corrib is the second largest lake in Ireland, though you might not think so, for it is so cut up by bays and promontories, and so strewn with islands, that the full extent is never apparent. Its complexities are familiar to the salmon that come up river under the Salmon Weir Bridge in Galway town to spread and to breed in familiar waters, where anglers seek to catch them. Salmon-fishing is popular on Loch Corrib, and it is free. There are people who come every year, not for the grandeur and the beauty of the mountains, not for the wonder and colour of the lakes and the sea, not for the character and manner of life of the people, though they may give perfunctory attention to these things as the necessary frame of their interest: they come to spend chilly hours on a boat on a loch, or by a loch shore, hoping to catch the marvel and beauty of a fine salmon as he rushes desperately at the end of a line in a glitter of broken water.

From the seventeenth century the principal families of Galway town were known as 'the tribes of Galway'. They lived confined within their town wall, with its fourteen gates, fearing the O Flahertys and other Gaelic tribes, but as time went on they began to emerge and to build houses for themselves beside the delectable lakes, as did, for example, the Blakes at Menlough on the east bank of Loch Corrib. Menlough looks picturesque in the tree-scattered county when seen across the water from the region of Moycullen, but it is, as might be expected, a ruin. The hamlet at its gates is quaint, with its white-walled, thatched cottages, where two youths fiddling with a powerful Japanese motorbike seemed a startling anachronism. The little gateway to the derelict castle drive, now a mere lane, is a folly, a stagelike miniature castle façade. Menlough itself began as a fifteenth-century tower-house, to which subsequent additions were made; it was accidentally burned out in 1910.

Claregalway, north-east, has ruins of a castle of the Burkes and of a Franciscan friary founded in 1290 and extended in the fifteenth century. As was often the case in Ireland, the friars were not convinced by the Reformation, nor by Cromwell either; they stayed on here until 1765. The walls stand to the eaves and a graceful tower rises from them. I have not been able to solve a minor puzzle in this friary: an old headstone has the word 'wife' carved upside down in relation to the rest of the inscription.

North-east, and still in the limestone country, is Abbeyknockmoy, with the ruins of a monastery standing among fields in season yellow with the flowers of flags. The abbey, which was Cistercian, was founded in 1190 by Cathal O Connor of the Red Hand, King of Connacht. The ruined church has interesting carved monuments and what is remarkable, medieval wall-paintings; or they would be remarkable if you could see them, for they are open to the elements and have faded so that they are visible only in certain conditions of the light. I am assured that they are there.

Northwards we come to Tuam, a cathedral town for both the Catholic and Protestant persuasions. The local people pronounce it as 'Choom'. The Catholic cathedral of St. Jarlath recalls by its dedication the foundation of a monastery by that saint in the fifth or sixth century; but the cathedral itself is an ornate neo-gothic building of 1837. In the twelfth century the O Connor kings of Connacht made the town their centre and from this period there remains an interesting but reconstructed high cross, with a wheel-head and a carving of the Crucifixion.

The Protestant cathedral is also basically twelfth century, with a wide and splendid chancel arch of rosy sandstone, lavishly carved, and backed by similar carving of the narrow east windows, on one of the splays of which the Devil is to be seen pulling Adam's ears.

At Kilbennan, two and a half miles to the north, is a broken round tower. From Tuam we take the road westwards towards Headford, passing about half-way the enchanted hill of Knockmaa, an isolated summit of 552 feet, on which is a cairn said to be the burial-place of Ceasir, who led the first inhabitants of Ireland. The hill is also the home of Kinvarra, king of the fairies.

Headford, in countryside divided by stone walls, has several times won the Bord Fáilte award for its neatness and order. The surrounding countryside contains the remains of several Norman castles, as at Moyne, Kinlough, Shrule, Cargin, Annaghkeen, and Ballycurrin, and of ancient churches at Donoughpatrick, Kilcoona, Cloghanover, Cargin, Killursa, Moyne, and Kinlough. Killursa was founded in the early seventh century by St. Fursay, a saint given to visions, which, it is suggested, inspired Dante. He was born on Inchiquin in Loch Corrib, and in those islanded waters ardent fishermen might find rewards in the brown trout for which Headford is noted.

The parents of Oscar Wilde, Sir William Wilde and his wife – she wrote under the name Speranza – lived at Moytura House (a plain house, still private) by the north-east corner of Loch Corrib. Sir William was an enthusiastic antiquary who convinced himself and sought to convince others, that one of the two ancient battles of Moytura, a legendary encounter between the Fir Bolg and the De Danaans, was fought on the plain of Moytura nearby. Modern scholars doubt this assertion. In this rather scatty household of Sir William and Speranza, their extraordinary son Oscar Wilde was brought up.

The abbey of Cong

Cong is really in Mayo, but as the county boundary is close to the village it is convenient to deal with it here. The name means an isthmus, and Cong in fact stands on the isthmus dividing Loch Corrib and Loch Mask. The two lakes are connected by a river that flows in part underground and forms various caves. There is also a canal, well built, with a lock to overcome a difference in level; it was constructed during the famine to give work and wages to a hungry people. It was completed in 1850, but when water was admitted, with what ceremony was appropriate, it disappeared straight into the porous limestone and the canal has been mostly dry ever since. No boat has ever sailed from Mask to Corrib.

Around the village there are diverse views of the two lochs, of the plains to the east, and to the west of the mountains of Joyce's Country, whose outlier, Ben Levy, rises to 1370 feet on the isthmus itself. The village is a noted angling centre, and indeed in a shop we entered, which, as is the way of Irish country shops, sold tobacco, sweets, porter, soda bread, bacon, drapery, and other things, half a dozen fine trout, newly caught, lay displayed on a spread newspaper.

The village centres round a dumpy cross of stone. The shaft is a restoration, the base medieval, with an inscription asking for prayers for two abbots of Cong. A few steps away, towards the bridge, a stile leads to Leac na bPoll, that is 'the stone of the hole', or of the holes. It is a five-basin bullaun, possibly connected with the earlier religious foundation of Cong. A bullaun is usually a natural boulder with one or more artificial basin-like hollows formed in its surface. Many people have suggested that these hollows were used as mortars for the grinding of grain, some have said they were fonts. What is sure is that there are hundreds of bullauns around the country in the ruins of monasteries and churches.

A monastery was founded at Cong in the seventh century by St. Feichin. It became a favourite place of Irish kings, some of whom are buried here. The last of them, Ruairi O Connor, spent the declining years of a sad life in the calm of the abbey until his death in 1198. The descendant of the O Connor high kings, the O Conor Don, still has a house in Ireland, at Clonalis in the neighbouring county of Roscommon. He is a Jesuit priest.

The abbey was rebuilt in the twelfth century as an abbey of the Canons Regular of St. Augustine. Unfortunately not much remains of this rebuilding, and nothing of the previous Celtic buildings of St. Feichin. A beautiful transitional doorway not far from the market cross, in the centre of the village, leads into part of the Abbey church, and beyond this there are three splendid doorways leading to the cloister. These are enough to show that the stonemasons of Cong were of the very first class and to indicate the quality of the parts of the abbey that are lost to us. The ranges of the cloister show rather the restoring hand of Sir Benjamin Lee Guinness and the mason he selected for the work was no bad choice. Peter Foy and other members of his family showed what they were capable of and how craftsmen of the nineteenth century could sensitively handle the work of those of the thirteenth (*Plate* 5).

By the cloister an ancient hall with a serving-hatch was the abbey refectory; it has a curious chimney whose twisted shape is said to have been the result of a great wind that struck Cong in the night.

Follow the path past the refectory, by pleasant lawns and yew trees, and you come to a footbridge over one of Cong's clear limestone rivers that flows from here into Loch Corrib. By its side is a small roofless stone structure standing out over a channel of the stream, which flows beneath it. This is the monks' fishing-house. The monks are said to have had a trap here for fish, and when a fish was caught in it – a fine salmon or a trout perhaps – its struggles caused a bell to ring in the monastery kitchen to tell the monks that their Friday dinner had arrived.

The abbey held a precious relic, which would have been the cause of its evident prosperity. This was a fragment of the True Cross, no less. No matter that there were probably sufficient fragments of the True Cross in the world to make up half a dozen entire crosses, people of the time were credulous and gave their faith and their alms to the fragment at Cong, and no doubt it enjoyed its share of miracles. The abbey enshrined it in a beautiful and elegant processional cross of oak covered with plates of silver and bronze washed over with gold. At the centre of the cross where the arms intersect, a boss of crystal covered the fragment of the True Cross. This processional cross, called the Bachall Buidhe (the yellow crozier), was made in county Roscommon by a consummate artist in metal, and his name has survived as it deserves to. He was Maoiliosa Echan, and he worked to the orders of King Turlach O Connor, for whom an inscription on the cross asks a prayer.

With what pride the abbots of Cong carried this precious cross in processions of the monks through the town! Such huge processions, some of them! Irish monastic houses are often spoken of as housing great numbers, beyond belief. Cong is said at times to have enclosed three thousand religious, a figure you could not suppose on the evidence of what remains.

The abbey was ordered to be dissolved by Henry VIII in 1542, and so large and powerful an abbey could not disobey as many a small priory did. As the abbot led his monks out of the building for the last time, and out of the village, they met a funeral coming in. The abbot made a crude cross out of two sticks and set it up on a pile of stones in honour of the dead. A custom of setting up little crosses at the entrances to the village is still followed. In three places (one in the Ashford demesne by the 'road of the corpses') you may see these 'croisíní' (cresheens) or little crosses decorating piles of stones.

The monastery was no more, but abbots of Cong lived on until 1829, their principal duty the guardianship of the precious Cross of Cong. The cross then apparently came into the possession of the parish church. When the great storm of 1839 – the night of the big wind – distorted the chimney of the abbey refectory, the roof of the parish church was damaged. In order to get funds to repair his church the priest sold the cross for a hundred guineas to Professor Mac Cullagh, who gave it to the National Museum in Dublin, where it still is. A later priest of Cong felt aggrieved by this sale and the alienation of the cross from Cong, and one day he came to Dublin, smashed the glass of the museum showcase, and stole the cross. He was promptly seized and the cross was restored to its display case.

The Catholic church of Cong was built in conventional gothic style in the nineteenth century, with three colourful stained glass windows by the Harry Clarke studios, and this was the church I saw when I first came to Cong. But when I came again in 1976 the Victorian church had been replaced by an original design that, because it was based on the use of flat asbestos sheets, was of a facetted outline. I thought it unusual and cleverly designed but because of the material supposed it to be temporary. The priest, Father Geraghty, tells me this is not so.

Opposite the Catholic church stands the roofless shell of the former Anglican church, with blackberries growing in its chancel. The present Anglican church stands in Ashford Castle demesne.

The gate to the demesne is at the end of the street near by. You may catch a glimpse of the castle from various places, as from the bridge near the monks' fishing-house, but you may see it better by going yourself into the demesne – there is a small charge only for admission – to a very beautiful estate with rivers, lakes, and uplands. The very attractive hotel building stands in a demesne of about three thousand acres, covering most of the width of the isthmus between Mask and Corrib. The castle is based on a tower-house built in the eighteenth century by the family of Browne, one of the tribes of Galway. It was for a time the home of Lord Oranmore. Later it passed to the Guinness family and was extended by Sir Benjamin Lee Guinness, whom we have already met restoring Cong abbey. Sir Benjamin's son took the title of Ardilaun, from the name of a wooded island in Loch Corrib, Árd Oileán, High Island. He extended the house still further. It is now an hotel and the greater part of the demesne belongs to the Irish government.

Could you afford to stay at so wonderful a place? Ashford castle is not cheap, but its charges are what you might expect from an hotel of the first class. In 1978 a double room with a full breakfast cost £24.40 and dinner was £8.70. For that, for twenty-four hours, you may live like a lord.

In the hollow interstices of the limestone that makes up the isthmus of Cong there are many caves, with various degrees of accessibility. The Pigeon Hole a mile west of the village is reached by a flight of sixty-one rough steps descending to a rapid river. Ballymaglancy Cave, a mile farther away, penetrates 1,700 feet and farther underground, and it has stalactites and stalagmites, but it is perhaps more for the enthusiastic pot-holer or speleologist than the ordinary tourist. The Priests' Hole was a hiding-place for priests in the days of the Penal Laws, when to be a priest was a perilous occupation. Captain Webb's Cave is a pot-hole where Captain Webb, a ladies' man if ever there was one, disposed of his cast-off mistresses to the number of twelve. The thirteenth, wanting to be different, pushed *him* down the hole. It is one of a number of pot-holes with nothing special to distinguish it. Perhaps the most pleasant of the caves of Cong is Teach Aille (the house of the cliff), where a wide opening near the abbey descends to a stream of clear water, from which the monks are said to have drawn their water supplies – though why they should have bothered when a pleasant river ran by their fishing-house I cannot tell.

The stream through the Pigeon Hole is said to contain two white trout, which are a handsome youth and a beautiful maiden transformed into fish long ago, one of many such stories in the fairy legends of Ireland. It is no use your casting a line to catch these trout – they never take the bait. But a soldier did once try and succeeded. When he proceeded to grill his catch a young girl suddenly stood before him and pleaded with his so movingly that even a hard-hearted soldier relented and restored the girl to her lover in the cave. The fish has ever since borne a mark on its side, the scar of the hot pan.

Clonbur to Maam Cross

Clonbur lies in the centre of the isthmus between Loch Corrib and Loch Mask, and with these two great lakes so near at hand the village is naturally a fishing-centre. Immediately to the west rise the mountains of Joyce's Country, wild summits of gneiss and schist that reach 1900 feet on Bunacumeen above the beautiful Loch Nafooey, and look over to the 2207 feet of Maumtrasna to the north and to the Maumturks and the

Twelve Bens to the south and west. We are on the edge of the tumbled ranges of Connemara, but for the present we shall do no more than skirt them on our way back to Galway town. Joyce's Country is named after a race of Welshmen who settled in this remote district after the de Burgo conquest of Connacht in the thirteenth century.

Westwards from Clonbur the L101 crosses the head of the slender peninsula of Doorus extending into Loch Corrib, and runs alongside and above an inlet of the lake, with the bold amd imposing mass of Leckavrea Mountain ahead. Down in the lake an old castle rises from an island. This is Caisleán na Circe, or Hen's Castle, reputed to have been built by a witch for an O Flaherty, to whom she gave a magic hen, with the promise that the castle would never be taken so long as the hen lived. But in a time of siege O Flaherty ate the hen, with the result that was to be expected.

The Joyce's river extends back along a wild and glorious glen into the mountains and a road climbs along the river's course, passing the village of Maum to ascend over a pass below Devilsmother to Leenaun and the head of Killary Harbour; but we leave this at Maum where a road turns south across the valley between Leckavrea Mountain and a series of small lakes to Maam Cross.

Maum village is not very large – a house facing the road-junction and one or two more houses, and that is all. Below the junction the road crosses over the Failmore river by Teernakill Bridge. It is worth pausing on this bridge for the view upstream into the Maumturk Mountains towards the heights of Letterbreckaun, which, if there is at all good weather, will surely draw you towards them, and their still summits sailing the blue sky. Up there a couple of miles or so in a pass many pilgrims climb, or used to, to find St. Patrick's bed and holy well. The pilgrimage or pattern takes place at the end of July. Beside Teernakill Bridge we encountered an English couple we had met in an hotel in Galway. Young and inexperienced walkers, they had thought that they might visit the bed and the well and penetrate through to Recess on the T71 road south of the mountains, a distance of seven or eight miles, and return to Maum to their car. They now sat somewhat disconsolately beside the road trying to dry their shoes and socks. They had got as far as the bed, which turned out to be no more than a hollow in the ground, but demonstrative of the fortitude of Irish saints and of St. Patrick in particular, but they had blundered into peat bogs and got themselves thoroughly soaked. 'How could there be so much water' they said, plaintively, 'when the weather has been dry for days?' It puzzled them that on a hillside the water did not roll down and leave the ground dry.

Their adventures underline the frequently repeated advice to wear suitable clothing when climbing a mountain and to find out at least something about the route before tackling it.

You might suppose from the many occasions on which you will encounter the name of Maam Cross that it must be at least a town, but in fact it is no more than a hamlet of a few houses, a petrol station in the forecourt of a simple bar, and a large sign giving the names in Irish and English and the directions of as many places as could be got into the ample space available. For if Maam Cross is not in itself very much, it is a cross-roads that sooner or later brings every traveller in the west to this place. Northwards goes the road by which we have come from Maum, which gives access to Westport, Achill, Newport, Castlebar, and all the north-west; westwards are Clifden and Connemara; east and southward is a road through Oughterard and Moycullen to Galway.

All these are roads of delight, roads not for racing over in order to get to the other end; for mountains rise in the view, beyond the leaning rushes of the verges, mountains on which the sunlight gathers in glens and corries and is accompanied by blue shadows against which the white walls and dun thatch of an occasional cottage show on another plane, as in a Paul Henry painting – Paul Henry, an Ulsterman who died in 1951 after years of blindness, was a fine interpreter of the landscape and the country people of the west of Ireland.

Maam Cross to Galway

The T71 from Maam Cross passes through dark country splintered by a glitter of lakes, and sidles alongside the longest of them, Loch Bofin, to drop down into Oughterard, just above the point where the fishful Owenriff enters Loch Corrib. There is nothing in particular about Oughterard, except for the countryside and the lakes – and the fish, if you are an angler – but you will often encounter the name and you might as well pronounce it properly – not 'Awterard' as the English visitor tends to say, but 'Ook terawrd'.

From the cross-roads in the town a wild little road runs north along the lake shore, on a ledge of Keeraunageeragh, to come to a stop at Curraun, opposite a point where an arm of Loch Corrib (that inlet containing Hen Castle, which we saw from the other side), faces the wooded hill of Doon across the water.

As you return, the broad expanse of Loch Corrib lies before you, with its islands heightened by trees. Inchagoill, the 'island of the devout stranger', has ancient ecclesiastical remains.

Two miles south-east of Oughterard a signpost beside the T71 indicates a lane leading to the castle of Aughananure – cars may go as far as a convenient car-park. Aughananure was an exceptionally fine tower-house, said to have been built by a de Burgo in the thirteenth century, but reconstructed in the fifteenth century as a stronghold of the O Flahertys, who were feared so much by the tribes of Galway. A fragment of the bawn remains, including two ornamented windows, all that stands of a fine hall that long ago collapsed into a stream below, over a cavern of which the hall had been built (*Plate* 6).

In the days of the castle's prosperity the floor of the hall was, according to legend, made on purpose to be collapsible. One of the flagstones was hinged downwards like a hangman's trapdoor. An unwelcome guest could, against his knowledge, be seated on a chair on this trap and, when his host decided was the time, might, by the simple drawing of a bolt, be precipitated into the water and the dark below. O Flaherty is reputed to have played this unpleasant trick on a de Burgo sent to ask for rent due for the castle. Afterwards he decapitated the body and sent the head to the young de Burgo's father. 'From the fury of the O Flahertys good lord deliver us'!

Ross House, some miles south beside the shore of Ross Lake, was the home of the Martins, until the famine one of the wealthiest families in the west of Ireland. Violet Martin was born in the house in 1862; she was the 'Ross' of Somerville and Ross – Somerville was her cousin, Edith Oenone Somerville of Castletownshend in county Cork. Together they wrote a series of novels and short stories the best-known of which is the collection called *The Reminiscences of an Irish R. M.* Their humour, conceived from an ascendancy point of view, is not appreciated by all Irishmen, but I find their stories frequently hilarious.

Colourful Connemara marble is quarried near Moycullen. It is used for a large range of trinkets and ornaments, which are sold in a shop in the village.

The main road goes on to Galway town, with the mass of the cathedral coming into view from a long distance.

4
The city of Galway

The city of Galway, the metropolis of the west, stands astride the river Corrib on a strategic site. Look for a moment at the map. Galway is set at the north-east angle of Galway Bay. To the north the great chain of lakes extends for many miles, between the limestone plain of the east and igneous mountains that rise like fortresses in the west. The most convenient route from east to west avoids the lakes by crossing the brief little river Corrib, the river that conducts all the issue of the lakes to the sea. It will be seen on the map that modern roads converge on the crossing, a reflection of the ancient and continuing importance of the site. It was an obvious place for a castle, and according to the Annals of the Four Masters a castle was built there, which was afterwards several times destroyed and built again. Also here was a small fishing village called Ballinshruane. Round about were the lands of the O Flahertys, the O Hallorans, and other Irish septs.

The Normans were naturally attracted to the site, since it governed movement over a large area of territory, and despite treaties with the kings of Connacht, Richard de Burgo in the thirteenth century seized the river crossing and built a strong castle and a settlement. By 1278 Galway was a walled town, an island of Anglo-Norman rule and culture in the heart of an Irish Gaelic district, but so cut off from English influence and control that it became practically an independent city state. Its contact with the sea gave it an outlet and Galway flourished as a port.

The city was governed by a group of fourteen Anglo-Norman families, who dourly maintained their integrity through centuries; they were the families of Athy, Blake, Bodkin, Browne, D'Arcy, Deane, ffront, ffrench, Joyce, Kirwan, Lynch, Martin, Morris, and Skerret, names, as you will see, basically English. The most influential were the Lynches, who between 1485 and 1654 provided 84 mayors of the town.

When the Cromwellians came they found these families intact and, not recognising them as distinctly English as themselves, referred to them in derision as 'the Tribes of Galway'.

Throughout the middle ages the tribes feared attack by the Irish of Connacht (including the de Burgos, who had turned Irish as Mac William Uachtar Burke), and they formulated various edicts prohibiting or controlling the presence of Irish in the town, 'that neither O nor Mac should strutte ne swagger thro the streets of Galway'. Above one of the fourteen gates they placed the inscription 'From the fury of the O Flahertys good Lord deliver us'.

The town prospered in trade with the Continent, especially with Spain. Spanish influence was strong, and when a fire destroyed part of the town in 1473, the houses of the tribes were rebuilt to plans said to have reflected Spanish styles, with round-arched doorways and rooms arranged round an interior courtyard.

Galway's loyalty to the crown of England in the persons of the Stuarts caused it to be invested by the Cromwellian Sir Charles Coote, to whom it had to surrender in 1652. It was besieged again by Ginkel for William III in 1691. After that it fell into a long decline that was not arrested until the present century. It now has several industries, without being at all industrial in appearance, and is a notable centre of the tourist trade.

Many of the names of the tribes may be found in the telephone directory, but the families are no longer as prominent as they were. The town retains evidence of its ancient plan, but the town walls, with their fourteen towers and fourteen gates, have almost entirely disappeared. The first thing to catch the visitor's attention is the modern Eyre Square, once open land before Williams Gate, and now a paved square on a gentle slope. A remnant of the tribes stands isolated on the pavement at the upper end of the square: it is the main doorway, with a window above it, of a house of the Brownes, originally built in 1617 and re-erected here as an exiguous memorial of the past of Galway. Near it is the statue of a little old man, Pádraig O Conaire, in the worn clothes of a countryman; he was notable in the west for his short stories in Irish. The statue is by Albert Power. Another monument, an overwhelming solid block, commemorates the visit in 1963 of President Kennedy. In the hall of the National Bank on the south side of the square Galway's civic sword and mace may be seen. The sword dates from about 1610 and is covered with inscriptions, among which are references to the restoration of King Charles II and the accession of William and Mary. The mace was made in Dublin in 1710. When Galway corporation was dissolved in 1840 the sword and mace became the property of the last mayor, Edmund Blake. In 1935 they were bought by William Randolph Hearst and passed to America. Hearst expressed a wish that they should, at his death, be returned to Galway, and in 1960 they were brought back.

Leading from the top of the square, Williamsgate Street, continued by William Street and Shop Street, form the principal shopping thoroughfare of the town. At the junction with Abbeygate Street stands Lynch's castle, the house of the Lynch family, one of the fourteen tribes. Lynch's castle is a well preserved tower-house of the sixteenth century made spectacular and unusual by the application of various carved ornaments and armorial bearings in stone on the exterior walls. The tower-house, now part of the offices of a bank, contains an interesting exhibition concerning the history of the building. Lynch's castle is the sole example of the houses of the tribes to survive in so complete a condition, but an observant walk through the back streets of the town will reveal other remnants – the corner of a tower embedded in a later structure, or examples of carved stone above doorways. Lydon's restaurant, in Shop Street, has several examples of carved stones and window surrounds applied to the interior walls. (*Plate* 3.)

Abbeygate Street leads to Market Street, where part of a house built into the churchyard wall of St. Nicholas's church commemorates a tradition of Galway and the Lynch family. The Lynch memorial window, as the fragment is called, is supposed to have played a part in a tragedy that occurred late in the fifteenth century, when James Lynch Fitz Stephen was mayor. His son Walter in a jealous rage murdered a young Spaniard, a guest in the mayor's house. Walter was condemned to death, but he was a popular young man and no-one would consent to do the office of hangman. The mayor therefore took an affectionate farewell of his son and hanged the young man himself from the window, in sight of the people and many of Walter's relatives. The story, it must be said, is of doubtful authenticity, but it has endured a long time.

The church of St. Nicholas of Myra, with three wide aisles, is the largest medieval church in Ireland. It was built in 1320, given its short tower in the fifteenth century (its pyramidal spire was added in 1683) and widened in the sixteenth century. The eighteenth century provided the gothick west window. As most medieval churches in Ireland are, it is Anglican, and as most Protestant churches are, it is likely, in my experience, to be often found closed and locked. But it is worth persevering to get inside. The sixteenth-century font bears the trefoil and lynx of the Lynch family, and there is a fifteenth-century stoup that is detached, like another font. The small chapel of the Blessed Sacrament, off the north aisle, is entered by a two-bay opening divided by a lovely and delicate spiral pillar, supporting cinque-foiled tracery. The piece does not seem to belong, but where it may have come from is not known. One of the openings is closed by a stone bar, and this has led some commentators to describe it as a confessional or part of a reader's desk from a monastery.

In the floor of the north aisle are several slabs with trade symbols – crowned hammers for goldsmiths, scissors for tailors, compass and square for carpenters, etc. An ornate sixteenth-century tomb, against the east wall of the transept, is said to be for a member of the Joyce family. Against the south wall stands the tomb of James Lynch Fitz Stephen, the man who is believed to have hanged his own son for murder.

Christopher Columbus is reputed to have attended a mass in St. Nicholas's church; perhaps he had come to Galway to investigate rumours that many centuries earlier St. Brendan had found land to the west. A Galway man, Rice or Penrise de Culvey, sailed with Columbus to the discovery of the Americas.

The Salmon Weir Bridge, built in 1819 and one of the sights of Galway, lies north of the church of St. Nicholas, the last bridge upstream before the Corrib river opens out into the loch. The parapet, which is a little high for leaning on, nevertheless shines from the polish conferred by the rubbing arms and clutching fingers of the many visitors who have peered over it and down into the swirling river in the hope of seeing salmon waiting in the pool below for a favourable moment to continue their journey up into Loch Corrib. At the right time of year (in spring) and in a good season hundreds of fish wait under the shadow of the bridge.

You can scarcely fail to miss the Catholic cathedral built on the west bank of the Corrib between 1959 and 1969, a building whose designer seems to have deliberately intended that it should above all be impressive and 'catholic' in the sense of eclectic, and has brought in a medley of architectural idioms to that end. He has certainly been successful in this aim. The cathedral guide-book says that the design of churches requires extensive reading and expert knowledge, and that is apparent here in an extraordinary mixture of styles, including a

Renaissance dome, round arches, gothic rose windows, and towers with what is said to be a Spanish influence. The cathedral is cruciform, with all four arms equal, broad and spacious, converging inside on a central altar under the large dome. There is a lot of Irish marble, colourful stained-glass windows, and notable stations of the Cross in carved stone in a spacious and airy interior.

Beyond the cathedral, University College is by comparison restrained, its older buildings by Joseph B. Keane in neo-Tudor collegiate style. It is a constituent college of the University of Ireland.

The Claddagh, on the west bank of the Corrib, was originally the Irish-town of the English city of Galway, outside the English walls and on the other side of the river Corrib. Until the nineteenth century it was highly individual, with its own customs and manners, and its men claimed the sole right of fishing in Galway Bay. The houses of the Claddagh were single-storey thatched cottages, picturesquely and irregularly placed, in a scene enlivened by the full red skirts of the women and the grey báiníns of the men. For the Victorian tourist the Claddagh was something to be seen, and to be entered with the thrill of trepidation. It has all gone. The Claddagh has for years been a grey-walled, dull council estate, its individuality lost or thinly diluted, its manners planed to the general level. There remains the Claddagh ring, a circle joined by two hands clasping a heart, which was used in Claddagh marriages – marriages that by custom were preceded by an elopement. Such rings can be bought in the shops in Galway.

Wolfe Tone Bridge crosses the Corrib to an open space hemmed in by crumbling warehouses. This was the fishmarket, where the men of the Claddagh came to sell their catch. To the right is a crude double arch, called the Spanish Arch, the only remaining gate of the walls that anciently surrounded the city, taking its name from the former trade with Spain. It leads through to the Long Walk, which has a quay beside the river, where small ships and boats berth. In the river in early summer, by old custom, salmon are netted. At other times fleets of swans gather.

East of the Long Walk are the New Docks, with some industrial buildings and the berths from which ships leave for the Aran Islands. Docks Road goes on and takes a corner into Eyre Square.

5
The Aran Islands

No part of the west, no part of Ireland, so distinctively impresses the visitor as the islands of Aran. Though in fact many points of the mainland lie farther west, Aran appears as the ultimate, the farthest outpost, inhabited by a race apart. Visitors from other countries seem to expect a way of life on the islands unchanged and primitive, preserving into the late twentieth century an age long gone by. If they have seen Robert Flaherty's magnificent film *Man of Aran*, made between the wars and occasionally revived – you may see it on Aran, in the Halla Rónáin – the parish hall at Kilronan on Inishmore, which also serves as a cinema – they will have a false idea of what Aran was like within living memory. Flaherty chose to present an Aran of at least a hundred years before his time, with the islanders precariously hunting in currachs for basking-sharks, and harpooning them in the open sea. In fact Flaherty could find no-one on Aran who had any experience of this hunt, and he had to import some of his fishermen from Achill, where this industry is still practised. But do not let this deter you from seeing the film in the Halla Rónáin at Kilronan. Most of the actors taking part in it were people from the islands.

The Aran Islands lie across the mouth of Galway Bay some thirty miles from Galway town, but much nearer to the mainland across the South Sound to the coast of Clare or across the North Sound to Gorumna Island, which is linked by bridges to the coast of Iar-Chonnacht. Aran comprises three islands in a line, with the small Brannock Islands in addition at the north-west end. Inishmore, the largest of the islands, about eight miles long, has its capital at Kilronan, facing Killeany Bay and out over Galway Bay. Inishmaan, the middle island, the island on which John Millington Synge stayed and found material for his plays *Riders to the Sea*, *The Shadow of the Glen*, and *The Playboy of the Western World*, is about three miles across. Inisheer, the southern island, is only about two miles across, but though the smallest of the three islands, it welcomes the visitor with the amiability of a broad and beautiful sandy strand.

The islands are geologically an extension of the limestone *karst* country of the Burren, share the same terraced construction, and share also much of the alpine and Mediterranean flora that distinguishes the Burren. On the east side the land slopes low to the sea, but towards the south and west it rises steeply as incredibly stony terraces to a height of 400 feet on Inishmore, and along the Atlantic aspect falls in sheer or underhung cliffs to a tumultuous ocean.

The islands may be reached by motor-boat from Doolin on the Clare coast or by cabin cruiser from Rossaveal on Greatman's Bay of county Galway, but the most usual route by sea is by ship from the harbour in Galway town. The *Galway Bay* of Córas Iompair Éireann, the State transport organisation, sails to Kilronan on Inishmore and allows day-visitors about six hours on the island. If that is not long enough – and it certainly is not long enough to make more than a brief visit to the nearer items of interest – you may certainly stay longer, in one of the many guest-houses or hotels – simple but civilised – to return on another day. Another boat, the *Naomh Éanna* (pronounced 'Nayv Aynna' – it means 'St. Éanna') also run by C.I.E., sails two or three times a week, and visits all three islands in turn. You will be well advised to check with a time-table before planning a visit to Aran. The journey to Inishmore takes about three hours to cover thirty miles of sea.

There are now also daily flights to Aran, landing at Killeany on Inishmore and also on Inishmaan and Inisheer. The flight time is twenty minutes, to which you must add the time it takes to get to the airport and the requirement that you check in thirty minutes before the flight.

Inishmore may be explored by pony and trap or sidecar – the latter is the more usual Irish name for what visitors to Ireland call a 'jaunting-car'. There is always a line of these vehicles waiting by the quay on Inishmore. Alternatively you may hire a bicycle – enquire at Kilronan.

The islanders

The people of Aran are cheerful, courteous, and dignified, and less insular than you might suppose, for many of these islanders have travelled to and have worked in Britain, Canada, and the United States, and elsewhere. Here at home, they live a simple but onerous life, making a little money from tourism, from the raising of cattle and an occasional ass – the pastures, though small and few, are noted for the sweetness of their grass – and from such minor industries as the knitting of Aran sweaters and cardigans, which, however, are now copied extensively in Ireland and in England. There is also a fishing industry – you may see the boats at Kilronan. There are also subventions from the government to help the islanders to preserve their Gaelic speech. (*Plate* 4.)

The islanders used to have a distinctive costume, which still survives in part. The men wear, over a thick shirt, commonly dark blue, a kind of heavy waistcoat made of unbleached wool and therefore whitish in colour; it is called a *báinín* (*bawneen*), from the Irish word for 'white', *bán*. In colder weather they have the thick Aran sweaters with distinctive patterns, knitted by the island women. With this garb go trousers of thick, heavy tweed, too ponderous ever to maintain a crease; these are held up by a patterned woven belt called a *crios* ('*kriss*'), the pattern distinctive of the family of the wearer. This outfit used to be topped by a broad-brimmed, shallow-crowned black hat or a knitted tam-o-shanter. On his feet the islander wore home-made raw-hide shoes called pampooties. The *báiníns* and the heavy trousers survive because they are practical in the hard weather that is frequently experienced on the islands, where, though there may be no frosts, rain and cold winds are common, but the rest of the costume is now rare; boots take the place of pampooties and ordinary flat caps are worn instead of the broad hats or tam-o-shanters of other days.

The island woman wore a thick, warm, fringed shawl thrown over the shoulders and drawn crosswise over the breasts; with this went a heavy skirt of red flannel descending to the ankles. The red skirt was the common costume not only of Aran but of the women throughout the west of Ireland. A second skirt was, in wet weather, drawn over the head like a cape, with the waistband about the face. The red skirt, whether about the head or in its normal place, is not now so often seen, even on Aran, but the warm and protective shawl, whether black or patterned, is too useful and too charming to suffer so easily a change of fashion, and even young girls going to mass on a Sunday may wear one. Long may they survive.

A version of the island costume may be seen on small boys, but the girls are more commonly dressed in a manner you might expect to see in a mainland town or in England – in other words, more or less conventional European fashion.

Many low, single-story thatched cottages may be seen on the islands but in recent years a number of modern bungalows and houses have been built. Some of these modern dwellings are used in season for the accommodation of visitors. Some are used for students of Irish, who come in the summer for several weeks to practise the language with men and women who have spoken it since childhood. All three islands are Irish-speaking and the common exchange of home and field and pub is in that tongue; but almost all the islanders speak English as well and will greet you in English if they have reason to believe that is your native speech.

Only a few trees are found on the islands, and these are cherished in gardens. There were probably never many trees growing wild, and the few there were would have sprouted from crevices in the limestone where the winds had lodged a little soil. The soil you now see in the little fields has been made by generations of farmers spreading seaweed, sand, and animal manure over the bare rock. Nor are there turbaries on the islands where fuel might be dug in the form of turf. One wonders how the evidently large population of ancient times managed to keep warm and dry on these wet and windy islands on the edge of the Atlantic. More recently, frequent loads of turf were brought over from the mainland in the small single-masted sailing-boats called hookers, which were once common around Galway. Turf maintained a perpetual flame in the wide hearths of the island cottages, under the iron vessels called corcáns and bastables, which were suspended over the fire from an iron crane and a chain. The cauldron-like corcán was for boiling water and cooking stews, the flat-bottomed bastable was used for baking the delicious flat cakes of soda-bread that were a staple of Irish meals. Soda-bread is still baked and eaten everywhere in Ireland, and regularly appears on breakfast tables and tea-tables in hotels, guest-houses, and farm-houses.

Turf fires have given way to coal from distant Cardiff. Cooking is now done more and more with modern gas-stoves fed by bottled gas. Electric light takes the place of candles and shark-oil lamps. Gas and electricity are certainly improvements, and no-one would want the Aran housewife to have to live without them; but the modern world becomes more uniform day by day. The superannuated corcáns and bastables, once mere rusting rubbish, are now eagerly bought by foraging gipsies and are sold as antiques by the roadsides on the mainland, to buyers who see in them a reminder and a remnant of a world gone by.

Modern civilization affects Aran as it does the mainland and with it comes the superabundance of tin-cans and packaging that is the bane of towns and villages. Combustible materials – paper and plastics – can be burnt, but for tin-cans there is nothing but the sea and it is painful to see a beautiful stretch of shore littered with cans in various stages of rust. At the house we stayed in our room overlooked a courtyard in which stood a splendid, modern bottled gas cooking-stove, which had arrived that day by boat from Galway. It was quickly installed in the house in place of an old-fashioned and superseded affair, which then stood in the courtyard for a couple of days. Later we saw this large piece of rubbish heaved over the sea wall, where it lay in a few feet of clear water until the storms of winter should remove it. The question of the disposal of rubbish is one that demands attention in any modern Arcady!

Visitors to the islands are sure to see currachs in use, the lightweight, frail-looking craft fashioned principally of laths and canvas and tarred over to produce a glistening black carapace that, as we have already pointed out, has often been likened to a huge black-beetle; when the boats are laid upside down on a beach or on a pier or quay, as they often are, the comparison is irresistible. The structure of a currach may resemble that of a Welsh coracle, and obviously the name is related, but otherwise there is little similarity. A Welsh coracle might not get farther than the river Teifi, but a currach is a sea-going boat, with a straight stern and a sharply pointed bow, which can live and float in rough water. A currach generally carries a crew of three, each man with two long, bladeless oars, which swivel on thole-pins, the pin fitting in a hole in a triangular piece of wood attached to the oar. A larger currach carries a crew of four. Sometimes outboard engines are fitted, or, rarely now, a sail.

Passengers on the *Naomh Éanna* to Inishmaan or Inisheer will encounter currachs first-hand, for there is no deep-water quay at either of these islands, and the ship must lie half a mile off-shore to transfer people and goods to these canvas boats. Those who have never before travelled in a currach are bound to be nervous of venturing in these craft as they bounce up and down beside the iron platform lowered down the side of the ship, but the bustle of crews and boats, the movement of the sea, and the conversation in Irish shouted from currach to ship tend to keep the mind occupied. The currachs are stronger than they look and their crews evidently capable. Amazing quantities of goods are brought out of the ship's hold and are ferried ashore in the currachs. Huge bottles of gas, sacks of cement, fertilisers, mattresses, sheets of hardboard, and many cartons are carried to the islands. In turn the produce of the islands is carried to the ship. Pigs and sheep go with their feet muffled in sacks or old coats to prevent their sharp trotters from piercing the canvas bottom of the boat. Horses, cows, and donkeys are dropped into the sea and are towed behind the currach with their heads held up by a man in the stern.

You will see from these remarks that a currach is a working boat and its seats may therefore not be impeccably clean. It is a good idea if you mean to go in a currach to take a newspaper or something of the kind just to sit on.

On Inishmore the *Naomh Éanna* and the *Galway Bay* berth at a quay and you walk ashore on a gangway; but the discharge and loading of cargo, with animals winched on and off, and the conspectus of the trade of the island, still make an interesting study.

Once on shore, you will need somewhere to stay. Except in the tourist season you may have difficulty, but if you are wise you will have booked accommodation in advance. The Bord Fáilte office in Galway will arrange this for you for the price of a telephone call – but give them advance notice if you can.

The forts

The islands are stuffed full with antiquities and no short visit will do to see even a tithe of them. The most important and the most fascinating are huge stone forts or cahers, of which there are several, built no-one knows when, nor against what foe – yet they must have been strong and forceful foes who could prompt such massive defences, just as they must have been desperate, numerous, and resourceful defenders who could build them, defenders organised under able chiefs. Most famous of these forts, and most commonly illustrated and described, is the one called Dún Aengus or Dún Aonghusa. Its several concentric ramparts, 18 feet high and nearly 13 feet thick, form a semi-circle with the two ends terminating on the edge of a cliff that falls nearly four hundred feet to the sea. Some argue that the fort was once a complete circle or oval, but I do not think so. I cannot believe that anyone would have erected walls along the edge of a cliff when the cliff itself formed so efficient a defence. (*Plate* 7.)

One of the defences of the fort was a *chevaux-de-frise* or *abatis*, a belt of sharp spars of stone set closely in the ground, such as we saw at Ballykinvarga in Clare. If you would emulate the experience of an invader, try negotiating this ankle-snapping obstacle, and consider that while you are busy picking your way through it the defenders would be lobbing sling-stones at you and peppering you with arrows.

Huge and strong as they may be, it appears that none of the forts of Aran was intended to withstand a siege, for none of them has a supply of fresh water.

Tradition suggests that Dún Aengus was built by the Fír Bolg, the 'men of the bags', whose chief was Aonghusa. Perhaps from the similarity of the name, some people equate the Fír Bolg with the Belgae, but Irish tradition includes elaborate legends about them and their origins. The Fír Bolg, they say, conquered Ireland before history began, and were themselves conquered, in battles on the mainland, by the De Danaan, a race of magicians. The Fír Bolg, it is said, retreated to the islands of the west and there laboured to build their stone forts. Fír Bolg, De Danaan, and their battles, with the building and defence of the forts, rest in an impenetrable murk of myth that is unlikely to yield precise fact.

Not far from Dún Aengus stands the circular fort of Dún Onaght or Dún Eoghanachta, with walls sixteen feet thick and sixteen feet high; near Kilronan is the double-walled Dún Eochla; and south of it again, on the cliff edge, is Dubh Chathair, the 'black fort', a promontory fort no less impressive than Dún Aengus, though some of it has gone over the cliff. Any one of these would be enough to distinguish Aran in the mind of an antiquary, yet there are additional forts on the smaller islands, including the magnificent and savage fort of Dún Chonachubhair, or Dun Conor, on Inishmaan, with its great walls built of cyclopean stones, as though by a race of giants; it is the largest, and perhaps the oldest, of the forts on Aran. On the highest point of Inisheer is Dún Formna, with a sixteenth-century O Brien castle inside it.

Aran of the saints

With the coming of Christianity and St. Éanna or St. Enda, pagan Aran became Aran of the saints. St. Éanna founded a monastery at Killeany on Inishmore in A.D. 483. Devout men flocked to it, to live their lives in the narrow confines of clocháns and to worship in the tiny, steep-roofed stone church; and from there some of them, like St. Ciarán and St. Kevin, left to found monasteries of their own. In the liberal enthusiasm of the early Celtic church many of the followers of Éanna were accounted saints themselves – a hundred and twenty of them lie under the blown sand around Éanna's little church, which still stands, though a ruin, at Killeany. The ruin is that of a building of several periods, its steep gables overlooking an interior only 24 feet by 15 feet. Parts of the walls are of huge stones and these parts are the oldest, possibly built by St. Éanna himself.

There are other old and evocative ruins on Aran. On Inishmore, for example, there is Teampall Bheanáin, the church of St. Benignus, a tiny building thrusting its naked gables skywards from the top of a stony hill above Killeany. Below it, in line on the hillside, lie the butt of a round tower and the stump of an ornate cross-shaft. Near Kilronan and Dún Eochla stands the larger, and later, church of Ciarán, possibly of the ninth century, and not far away is Teampall Assurnaidhe, the church of St. Sourney, the fifth-century nun whose name we have already met at Drumacoo on the mainland. Farther along the twisting spinal road of the island towards Kilmurvey, the delightfully named Teampall an Cheathrar Álainn, the church of the four handsome ones, stands where the limestone ridges slope up towards Dún Aengus and the view extends over the waters of Galway Bay rimmed by the peaks of the Twelve Bens – few of the ruins of Aran are not endowed with marvellous and panoramic views. The handsome saints were Conall, Berchán, Brendon of Birr, and Fursey. They lie under four large, plain flagstones outside the church, and near by are the remains of a number of clocháns, corbelled, circular stone huts, sometimes called 'beehives', such as those in which the saints and their followers would have dwelt. Also to be seen are a holy well and a bullaun.

Farther on, beyond Clochán na Carraige, the clochán of the rock, a large and intact 'beehive' hut, you will find the Seven Churches. 'Seven' here is the usual magic number; there are in fact only two churches – Teampall Bhreacáin or Brechan's church, and Teampall an Phoill, the church of the hollow or of the hole – together with monastic buildings, all within an enclosing wall. Teampall an Phoill is a fifteenth-century building, of no special interest, but the church of St. Brechan is early, perhaps of the ninth century, though altered since. In its grassy and hummocky graveyard are several ancient headstones, some of which show incised or relief crosses. The ruin of this little community, low on the island and near the shore, crouched from the winds of the west, seems still to be instinct with devotion and prayer.

The many ruins – of ancient forts, of churches, of the Elizabethan fort of Arkyne at Killeany – are linked by wandering roads. Stone is everywhere, the misty, ghostly stone wrenched from the limestone or simply gathered to clear a space and for no better reason piled into dry-stone walls around table-cloth fields. The dry-stone walls may appear bizarre, built so loosely that there may be more space than stone, a reticulation of rough spars through which the wind passes unimpeded; and this indeed is the idea, for the loose walls of Aran stand against the bitter blast of the west where a more closely set masonry would be pushed flat on its face. Then there is a peculiarity of Aran fields that you must take into account – many of them have no gates. Timber and iron for gates would have to be imported and would be expensive. So, a portion of wall is easily dismantled to let a cow or an ass go through, and the wall is built up after it. It is a homely detail derived from the stony context of these strange and wonderful islands on the edge of the western world, where the land rises from the low shores facing the mainland to the high cliffs that front the Atlantic. Standing on those perilous rims, with the advancing white waves far below like mere ripples, you may imagine America as the next landfall to the west, and perhaps strain to see the shining land of Hy Brasil that tempted St. Brendan and his friends, after receiving the blessing of St. Éanna, to put to sea in a currach and to discover distant countries and far marvels. More factually, you may look far to the south to see the dim hump of the saint's Mount Brandon in Kerry, the serried capes of the Cliffs of Moher in Clare, the shimmering grey land of the Burren, and to the north the summits of the Twelve Bens, with, perhaps, emerging from a shawl of mist, the holy mountain of Croagh Patrick in Murrisk in Mayo.

6
Iar-Chonnacht and Connemara

'Iar-Chonnacht' means 'West Connacht'. 'Iar-Chonnacht' is the hilly and lake-strewn country reaching westwards from Loch Corrib and north of and inland from Galway Bay. Upland country, much of it, but by no means mountainous, it is still remote and largely unfrequented even in this tourist-ridden twentieth century. The reason for this lies in its lack of roads. If you look at the map you will see that a district extending fifteen miles from Moycullen to Costelloe and from Spiddal up to Maam Cross shows little in the way of roads other than the wild and uppity road from Costelloe to Oughterard and the scarcely more frequented road from Spiddal to Moycullen. You will see that in coming from Maam Cross by way of Oughterard and Moycullen to Galway we have skirted this wilderness. As for other ways, there are little lanes and bohreens into the hills, more or less rough, and more or less uncomfortable for cars. These ways lead to some of the many lakes set in the granite hollows of the hills, lakes in which an angler may as often as not meet a welcome rendezvous with a brown trout, or with a sea-trout or a salmon that has struggled up one of the clear, cold rivers such as the Owenboliska, which meets the sea at Spiddal.

Tourists commonly head westwards from Galway, through Salthill, which is Galway's seaside suburb, with a long promenade facing across the bay to the distant hills of Clare. For miles the road follows beside the sea, either a little inland or close beside the shore. Indeed, from Barna west to Tully, where the road turns north beside Cashla Bay, this district on the borders of Iar-Chonnacht is known in Irish as 'Cois Fhairrge', which means 'by the sea' (pronounce it approximately 'Kesh Arraga'). For the first part, nearly as far as Spiddal, you may be disappointed with this stretch, especially if you had supposed it to be remote and wild. Many bungalows and houses have appeared in the last decade or two, forming an unwelcome strip development, and there are new buildings also on the seaward side, where there is room.

A few traditional thatched cottages, with white walls and dun thatch, remain, looking as though they belonged here where brick and tile are alien. Some of these little dwellings are smart and well kept, clearly done up as country retreats or second homes for citizens of Galway or points farther east, or perhaps to let for the holiday trade – the use of cottages as accommodation for holiday-makers is a growing business, as we shall see later. (*Plates* 4–12.)

Spiddal to Oughterard

Near Spiddal the road runs for a short distance beside the beach, and here, wandering among the interspersed boulders and patches of sand of the shore, I commenced a little collection of Connacht stones, a mini-museum of geology. It was inspired by the discovery of an attractive, sea-moulded, pinkish pebble of limestone, thickly peppered with small fossils, an erratic in this granite country, shuffled from elsewhere by the pull and tow of the sea, or even brought by a glacier ten thousand or a hundred thousand years ago. It persuaded me that with an observant eye I might find other, different stones of equal charm and interest wherever I went among the medley of sedimentary, igneous, plutonic, and metamorphic rocks that form the landscape, the cliffs, and the beaches of the west of Ireland. (*Plate* 19.)

There is not much of Spiddal – a little grouping of houses about the mouth of the Owenboliska, with a small hotel or two, an Irish college, and a Catholic chapel by Michael Scott, an original architect who, as Yeats found, too often wasted his talents in drink – we have already met him at Loughrea. Sarah Purser designed the four windows and also the opus-sectile or cut-tile stations of the Cross. Down by the little harbour, where you may see currachs, on a hillock surrounded by gravestones, stands a tiny, disused Protestant chapel erected in 1776 by 'Stephen Martin, gentleman'; it is still roofed, but the doorway and the window have been so thoroughly blocked up with cemented masonry that there is no way into it. The Martins were a rich and numerous family, practically rulers of this part of the west of Ireland, with their headquarters at Ballynahinch and Ross.

The road westwards runs a little inland from the sea, which laps a low shore, with the Aran Islands beyond, looking very close in fair weather, but retreating to a distant blur in the soft rain. Many hamlets and cottages are passed, until we come to Tully or An Tulach, where a small modern church rises on the seaward side of the road. The design is

simple and unpretentious, deliberately so, for this is a village church and
not meant to be grand. But enter past the baptistery into the simple hall
of the interior and look at the furnishings. The stained-glass windows,
with zig-zag patterns, fail in the theme of modesty and homeliness, but
the rest is beautiful and worth the journey all the way across Ireland. A
sculpted St. Columcille, the patron saint of the church, is attractive, but
the artist who has stamped his genius on Tully is Brother Benedict Tutty
of the abbey of Glenstal in county Limerick. Look especially at the altar
and processional crosses, the figure of the Virgin and Child in enamel on
beaten copper, and the enamel-and-copper stations of the Cross, and
perhaps you will regret that Brother Benedict Tutty was not given work
to busy his hands in the design and the furnishing of Galway's new
cathedral.

You may take the L100 directly north or loop round by the shore of
Cashla Bay, by lost little harbours to Rossaveal, from which a cabin
cruiser called *The Queen of Aran* runs regularly to the Aran Islands, which
appear over the breast of Galway Bay as a smudge on the distant rim of
the sea.

At a cross-roads on the L100 we meet a minor road tending north-
east. This is the one I have already mentioned, going over the hills to
Oughterard. A map of 1960 shows it as a track. Now it is surfaced all the
way, winding and undulating and going in company along the verges
with cohorts of rushes, which lean the way of the wind. There are many
lakes, shreds of water where keen fishermen come to find brown trout,
and bogs where men cut turves from the wet, shining little cliff faces of
the turbaries. They load the turves into creels on the backs of asses, with
a to and fro of conversation that has the patient, sweet quality of Irish.

From a high point of about 800 feet, near Loch Lettercraffroe, the
road descends as though it meant to drop into Loch Corrib, and you will
be breathless with the views of that splendid lake. And when you have
arrived at Oughterard, what then? Why, you have been in Ireland long
enough to be used by now to the tempo of Irish life, so go back again over
the road to Costelloe, past the anglers and the turf-diggers, never
minding the tourist imperative never to tread the same road twice.

Near Costelloe a lane is signposted to the Coral Strand. The strand is a
delightful place, with dark and shining rocks heaving from a beach of
brilliant white against a background of the serried mountains of
Connemara. But the beach is not sand. It is composed of fragments of a
kind of seaweed that develops a calcareous stem, and these fragments are

thrown up on the beach by the waves, which push them about among the black rocks with a noise like the sharp sound, a frou-frou of fine shingle. Take a quantity in your hand and you will see how it differs from sand. This is a very beautiful and memorable place, with the dead white coral contrasting with the clear emphasis of the dark rocks against the hazy background of the mountains and the green of the sea.

Beyond Greatman's Bay a series of bridges 'crosses the Atlantic' to connect a chain of islands. Lettermore comes first, and then Gorumna, which is larger, and then Lettermullen, beyond which fragments of land lie scattered in the sea in open water and in the enclosed Kilkieran Bay. The islands chained to the mainland are dark and sombre, with bare rocks emerging from the turf around little, indented lakes. They are not much visited by tourists, but there might be many more tourists if the reputation of these islands as 'poteen country' were more widely known. Poteen is illicit whiskey and the very fact that it is illicit – moonshine – gives it an attraction for the visitor, even though he may be law-abiding in his own country.

Poteen

Poteen certainly has been made in the islands, and probably still is, as it is in many other remote places in the west of Ireland, and made in considerable quantities. You may imagine a small still bubbling over a turf fire in a little white-walled cottage, stoked furtively by the man of the house while the children keep watch and the tell-tale smoke curls up into the air. Such small stills probably exist; but the moonshiners may be much more professional than that in an industry that is said to be worth more than half a million pounds a year. An organisation on Gorumna raided by the police in 1977 had several forty-gallon barrels of wash to feed two stills, the heat for which was provided by five six-foot-long gas containers. Perhaps the moonshiners had been too ambitious, for it must have been dificult to move all the equipment and the materials about the countryside in lorries, surreptitiously. The Gárdaí got wind of it and mounted a raid on the Gorumna still, which was sited on the edge of a lake. As one of the raiding party ran down among the boulders towards the still a collie dog barked a warning and two men, alerted by this, 'shot off' across the lake in a row-boat. The Gárdaí found barrels of mash, from which the poteen is distilled, hot and steaming and the two stills, dripping spirit into an enamelled bucket. The Gárdaí upset the barrels into the lake, and no doubt thereby inebriated the fishes, and they opened the valves of five large gas-containers and flung the containers into the water too, where, driven by the jets of gas, they veered about like demented torpedoes.

There have often been suggestions that the making of poteen should be legalised and controlled, and in the *Irish Times* of the 25th of January 1977 this idea is put forward again by Comhar Chumainn Cois Fhairrge, a Connemara trading co-operative. They say, in effect, that it is short-sighted to search for industries to come to the west and to ignore one that is already there and with a proven market. The council of the co-operative think that legalising poteen and controlling its manufacture would drive inferior and unacceptable qualities off the market and would protect the customer from some very rough stuff.

Poteen undoubtedly exists; but if you want to sample it you will have to find it and risk breaking the law in the attempt – the authorities are very down on poteen. The sample you find may turn out to be the worst, a near-poison made out of who knows what. Good or bad, it will be unlikely to exhibit any of the graces of long maturing. In fact you would be safer and would very likely more enjoy the experience if you sampled a bottle of Paddy whiskey from Cork and allowed its legal and friendly glow to warm your heart while you conjure up a picture of moonshiners tending their stills among the rocks.

Northwards the L100 goes to Screeb Lodge at the head of the sinuous and many-islanded Camus Bay, which is itself an inlet of Kilkieran Bay. Screeb may be passed without notice; it is renowned, as is Maam Cross, as a junction – for Joyce's Country and the Maumturks to the north and for Connemara and the Twelve Bens to the north-west. The L100 runs between the blue waters of Loch Ahalia and Loch Knockaunawaddy like a causeway bordered by rushes, to the lake country around Maam Cross. To the west of Maam Cross the prominent knob of the hill above Loch Ourid and Loch Shindilla beside the Ballynahinch road stands as a chip of the Maumturks, whose summits, rising to 2012 feet on Leck-avrea and 2193 feet on Letterbreckaun, border Derryclare Loch and Loch Inagh and face the Twelve Bens. Here is the heart of the mountains of the west, the wildest country, in which here and there a remote farm has been made in an unlikely place.

At Recess, little more than a name, an isolated shop sells decorative shillelaghs, sheepskins of beautiful quality, oddments of Connemara marble, thick shawls, trinkets, and Aran-knit wool wear, always popular – Aran báiníns have never achieved equal acclaim.

The Twelve Bens and Ballynahinch

Facing the shop across the road stands a Connemara-marble monument, like a piece of coloured crazy paving up-reared. Behind it was a lady's and gents' lavatory, an unlikely but welcome facility among these exposed roads. When I saw it first more than ten years ago it was new and clean and smart. After that louts wrecked it and smashed the windows and the basins.

Lissoughter, standing 1300 feet above Derryclare Loch and Loch Glendalloch, makes a picturesque group, with its pine trees, rocky slopes, blue waters, and the background of the Maumturks and the Twelve Bens, so well seen from the road that it has inevitably attracted artists and photographers by the score. You will recognise the view on the picture postcards sold in Roundstone, Clifden, and Leenaun, but these do not show that there are now electric cables and posts or pylons running straight across the foreground.

The Twelve Bens or the Benna Beola gather in a group of summits well over 2000 feet. The range forms an upland of high, roadless country stretching thirteen miles from east to west and six miles from north to south. Your two feet are the only means by which you may travel in this country – and be sure you are adequately clothed and well shod and knowledgeable or properly guided. All mountains are potentially dangerous and rescue parties are not as likely here as they may be for example, in England's Lake District or on Wales's Snowdon.

Below Ben Lettery on the north shore of Ballynahinch Lake An Óige has a Youth Hostel. On an island in the lake an ancient castle of the O Flahertys still stands as a reminder that this was O Flaherty country. It was Martin country too, for here at Ballynahinch a Martin, of one of the Tribes of Galway, ventured to build a house well away from the protection of the city. A descendant, Nimble Dick Martin, a clever lawyer with an eye to the main chance, founded a huge estate centred on Ross and Ballynahinch, which was enlarged to somewhere near a quarter of a million acres by the addition of O Flaherty land granted to the Martins at the restoration by Charles II – the Martins could boast that the road from distant Galway was bordered all the way by Martin property. A Later Martin gained the name of Humanity Dick from his interest in the welfare of animals, an interest that must have amazed the Irish countryman, who even today is not noted for his care of his beasts, much less of wild creatures. Some of the country people on Humanity

Dick's estate who offended against animals found themselves locked up for a term in the O Flaherty castle on the island in the lake at Ballynahinch, which became known as 'Martin's prison'. Martin braved ridicule to push acts through Parliament to protect cattle and horses and other animals from maltreatment. The famine, in which Thomas Martin and his daughter Mary spent a great deal in relief, broke the family fortunes and brought creditors down upon them. Mary died in New York.

The Martin house at Ballynahinch still stands on the south shore of the lake, an eighteenth-century mansion much altered and not improved in the altering. After being owned for a time by Prince Ranjitsinhji of Nawanagar – 'Ranji', famous as a cricketer – it became in 1945 an hotel – with keen fishermen among its clientèle. Many visitors come for the breathtaking views of the Twelve Bens across the lake.

The road goes on to Clifden, the sea, and the islands.

Turf and seaweed

Westwards from Screeb Lodge the L102 runs now and then close beside the water of Camus Bay and passes a power-station fed by the fuel that the Irish (who use it) call 'turf' and the English (who do not use it, except in gardens) always call 'peat'. It is for such stations that huge mechanical turf-cutters cut such enormous slices from the bogs. Ireland must one day – and perhaps soon – come to the end of its enormous supplies of turf.

Peat is formed under certain conditions of temperature and moisture, conditions that have prevailed in Ireland since the ice ages. Its influence has pervaded the economy and social life of the countryside, and even its atmosphere, for when it is used as a fuel turf gives off a sweet and penetrating odour that was characteristic of the countryside. It became for the exile the remembered scent that inspired his nostalgia to visions of cottages and mountains and the people and the speech of home.

But the scent of the smoke of the burning turf no longer pervades as it did. Although the countryman stills digs for turf in the bogs and stacks it in huge piles against the gable walls of his cottage, to feed his fires, more and more cooking is done with modern electric ovens or gas cookers fed with mains gas or bottled gas. The turf fire on the hearth loses some of its importance as the centre point of the family, the importance it enjoyed when everything – bread, meat, vegetables, and everything else – was cooked at the hearth on the glowing embers of turf with their margin of

1 Yeat's Thoor Ballylee

2 The Corrib valley from Moycullen, with Menlough castle

3 Lynch's castle in Galway

4 Aran Islanders meeting the Galway boat at Inishmaan

5 A carved capital at Cong

6 Aughananure castle

7 The entrance to Dún Aengus on Inishmore, Aran

8 Loch Nafooey

9 A primitive small cottage in Ballycastle

10 A cottage in Iar-Chonnacht, Galway

11 An iron-roofed cottage near Ballyconneely

12 Modern holiday cottages at Tully Cross

13 The *cruach* or summit of Croagh Patrick, with the pilgrim path

14 A mountain pass near Loch Fee

15 Doonbristy

16 Fishing in Sligo town

17 A turbary, with turves drying

18 Parke's Castle

19 Stones of the west: (a) water-rounded granite from Dog's Bay (b) mica schist from Belderg (c) Connemara marble (d) limestone pierced by coral stems, from Easky (e) veined marble (f) granite (g) limestone containing fossils, from Spiddal (h) breccia—various fragments in a matrix of sandstone, from Dog's Bay

20 The entrance gable of Creeragh church

21 Gathering seaweed at Bertraboy Bay

22 Roundstone harbour with the Twelve Bens beyond

23 Kildavnet castle, Achill

24 Stone circle at Carrowmore, with Knocknaree in the background

25 Enniscrone

26 Ballintober abbey

27 Flamboyant tracery at Strade

28 The Pietà at Strade: note the adoration of the figure on the left, the sensuous curves of the Magdalene, right, and the feathered angels

white ash. The turf fire might well have been burning for centuries, certainly for decades.

The cottager or the farmer usually owns or rents a turbary, a piece of land where turf may be dug from a layer of bog that may be several feet thick. He cuts a trench to form a vertical face, and then cuts against this to form neat sods all about the same size. He uses a special tool – a slane – which is a kind of spade, the blade having a right angle to cut two sides at once. You may notice that the long handle does not have a cross-bar like that of an Englishman's spade or fork, and here you have hit on something fundamentally different between the Saxon and the Celt. The long, straight spade handle like that of an Englishman's garden rake is found in all the Celtic countries – in Cornwall, in the Highlands of Scotland, and in Brittany, for instance, as well as in Ireland. The Englishman, used to his crossbar, cannot understand how anyone can dig without it, but the Celtic pole handle must have advantages, for the Celt's purposes, for it would not otherwise have persisted.

The straight lines and little cliffs of turbaries are to be seen in every bit of bog. Some of the turbaries are obviously ancient, worked out, and derelict, while others are clearly in use. A whole family will repair to a turbary to cut turf. While the head of the household and perhaps an adult son cut the sods and throw them with a twist up on to the bog surface, the women and the children collect them and arrange them in little stacks or stooks, like so many tiny dolmens, so that the air may blow through and dry them quickly. The particular pattern or method of these piles varies from district to district (*Plate* 17).

After a few days the sods may be turned to aid the drying. When the drying has gone sufficiently far the whole family shares in the job of carrying the sods to the edge of the road, where they are built up into stacks to await transport. Transport is commonly a horse and cart or an ass and cart, or it may be an ass with wicker panniers or creels slung on its flanks. The sods, probably enough for a winter's supply, are carried home to cottage or farm, where they are built up against the gable perhaps as high as the ridge of the house, or into a large stack nearby. This stack may be thatched.

Digging a supply of turf and bringing it home – 'saving it' is the term used in Ireland for this operation, as it is also for harvesting crops or hay – is very hard work.

A sod of turf, black or dark brown and fibrous, is not a prepossessing object, but it may be wealth for an Irish countryman. In a short poem I imagined such a countryman in the distant past encountering strangers, perhaps Phoenicians, landing rare and desirable merchandise on a lonely beach of the west of Ireland, and spurning the countryman's offer of an exchange.

> *Driving down from the turf bog in the rain*
> *he saw the broad boats drawn up on the strand*
> *and the queer dark men who, ankle deep*
> *in water, humped their bales on to the land,*
>
> *and lashed his ass all down the mountain road*
> *and offered turf for barter, turf to pay*
> *for silk and wine, but those dark men*
> *looked at his load and laughed and turned away.*

A side road turns off by the shore of Loch Aroolagh to run down a low peninsula between Camus Bay and Kilkieran Bay to Rosmuck, a scarcely perceptible little settlement. Here, on a ledge of hillside above a small lake, Patrick Pearse, the Irish patriot who signed his name to the Republic's proclamation in 1916 and thereby signed away his life, lived in a little whitewashed and thatched cottage and wrote plays and poems in English and in Irish. The cottage, now preserved and open as a national monument, is furnished as it was in his day, with at least one piece, an *art-nouveau* writing desk, that actually belonged to him.

Back on the L102 we follow west and south contouring the islanded Kilkieran Bay to come opposite Rosmuck to the village of Kilkieran. Here is the usual stony landscape of the west, with a few houses scattered here and there and seeming in the manner of villages in the west to have neither a nucleus nor a clear distinction from the next village. Inland there is a low range of hills with spectacular rocky sides, which I examined through binoculars while my car was being replenished with petrol. A road runs alongside the shore, and one soon notices extraordinary quantities of seaweed. The local farmers supplement the produce of their stony little farms by harvesting the seaweed out of the sea.

On shore they wade in the rich gooey weed and gather it up, or they take a boat off-shore and rake the weed into great rafts, which they call 'clemmings'. These they allow the tide to bring ashore. The seaweed is dried by a factory and is exported abroad to make alginates, which as I remarked at Quilty, are used in a number of food and beverage products.

You may also see the weed being collected by lorry, with parties of men building great stacks on board.

A shellfish research station was founded at Kilkieran to promote and improve the fishing for lobsters. The researchers breed the semi-translucent baby lobsters in tanks, and these creatures, only a few inches long but fully armoured and twice armed, like a medieval warrior, have a strange fascination, seeming to advance, even from first childhood, prepared to do battle against the world around them. Perhaps they are aware in their minds that their flesh within that shell is delicious to predators and especially to man. For him they have the value of an increasingly rare delicacy, and so are more and more valuable. Lobsters are not now as easily found and caught as once they were and so the research station was set up to investigate a product that is increasingly confined to the tables of expensive restaurants.

More common than lobsters are crabs, and crabs are caught off Kilkieran and processed in a factory that boils them and packs the meat for export.

Such activities as the breeding of lobsters and the production of crab-meat, as of many other small industries of the west of Ireland, are interests of Gaeltarra Éireann, a government agency, which exists to encourage new industries and revitalise old ones, to build factories in the west and to provide employment. You will find Gaeltarra-backed industries throughout the west.

A good deal of Irish is spoken in the Kilkieran district and you may hear it wherever the daily work of farm and sea is discussed; or in the evening in Peter O Grady's bar, where the locals and a visitor or two join in dancing and singing.

In June 1978 Kilkieran was the subject of a BBC television programme, which sought to give a view of Irish ways of life.

From Kilkieran we follow the L102 westwards towards Carna, skirting the shore of Mweenish Bay. A side road from Carna leads on to Mweenish Island. Out in the many-islanded sea lies St. Mac Dara's Island, where St. Mac Dara, demonstrating the usual search and preference for solitude characteristic of Celtic saints, founded a church and monastery in the sixth century. The church still stands on the eastern shore of the island, and there are carved early Christian decorated stones. Such was the reverence inspired by this saint that sailors were said to dip their sails three times as they passed the island. They may do so still, where sails still blow, but such traditions, customs, and superstitions are fading fast even in the far west of Ireland. What survives is often no more than a vague memory. Pilgrimages or 'patterns' to the island were long observed. If you would follow in the steps of those pilgrims you must seek a boat, probably in Kilkieran or Carna. You will at least enjoy, across the sea, a marvellous view of the mountains of Connemara and of the detached hill of Errisbeg above Roundstone, to the north.

Near Glinsk, in a land of boulder-strewn hillsides and eroded bays black with seaweed, men were piling a great mass of weed on to a lorry. Seaweed has for many years played a part in the economy of the west. Its simplest use nowadays is as a fertiliser on the land, but during the nineteenth century weed was gathered in great quantities and burned as kelp, an industry that marked the shores with numerous stone hearths and columns of smoke. Men and women, begrimed like creatures of Satan, gathered the weed and dried it for months before burning it and then stoked the bubbling mass. The ashes were sold to factories to go to produce iodine. Iodine was later synthesised and that was the end of kelp-burning and of a way of life on the shores and the islands of the west. Carraigín moss, a delicate, fern-like weed, is now dried and sold in packets to make an edible jelly. Dulsk and cranagh may be eaten raw – people buy them like sweets in paper bags and munch the weed in the streets. (*Plate* 21.)

Bertraboy Bay to Clifden

Bertraboy Bay extends deep inland to Cashel – not the Cashel with the famous ruined cathedral and round tower, which is in Munster – and we follow round the bay, sometimes at a distance, to Roundstone. Roundstone has its name from Cloch na Rón, the stone of the seal, and its English name is the result of misinterpreting the Irish language. Another example, near by, is Dog's Bay, a name that comes from Port na bhFeadóig, which means Plover's Bay. Roundstone is a pleasant little town designed in the nineteenth century by the engineer Nimmo, with a double row of houses, a church, and a pretty little harbour in which moored boats rock gently to the waves against an exciting background of the mountains of Connemara.

Errisbeag, rising to 837 feet above Roundstone, is a rough, mountainy hill of the kind of rock called gabbro. It is worth climbing for the marvellous views it offers of the sea and the islands, of the dark, lake-sprinkled district between here and Clifden, extending to the west to

Slyne Head, and of the graceful outline of the Twelve Bens. Dog's Bay and the neighbouring Gorteen Bay are seen to have been formed by an island offshore becoming connected with the mainland by a double curve of silvery sand: here are two of the most beautiful beaches in the west. In these bays I found two delightful stones, one a sea-rounded fragment of breccia, a collection of angular fragments in a matrix of sandstone probably of the Devonian period, and a handsome boulder of pink-speckled granite rolled into shape by 400 million years of tide and weather.

Ballyconneely is a slight village reached by a winding road above a rocky coast, a road that, because of the exhilaration of the air, is known as the Brandy and Soda Road – breathe as deeply as you can – the inebriation is free and untaxed!

Beside the extensive Mannin Bay near Ballyconneely is a Coral Strand, another delightful strand floored with the white, sand-like detritus of a coralline seaweed.

The road goes beside Mannin Bay to a side road that leads to the upland site of the Alcock and Brown monument. Here a large stone structure in the form of an airplane tail-fin points to the spot in Derrrygimlagh Bog, marked by a cairn, where Alcock and Brown's plane came down on its nose at the close of the first transatlantic flight in June 1918.

We descend to the town of Clifden, with its two tall spires and its picturesque situation at the head of Clifden Bay.

Clifden

Clifden is often called the capital of Connemara. The title is apt enough. and such events as the Connemara pony show, which takes place in Clifden, serve to confirm it, but it should not lead one to suppose that the place is large. It is simply the largest there is for some distance in any direction. Between here and Galway to the south and Westport to the north there is nothing much larger than a hamlet or the kind of scattered community that in the west may be called a village and possess a name, though it seems to have no centre and no defined edges, and is scarcely recognised as a village by visitors accustomed to the nucleated settlements of their own countries.

Clifden, however, is distinct enough, sufficiently so with its two prominent spires to have its own personality and a memorable outline. There is a selection of shops and a number of hotels and bars on its two wide main streets and the visitor need not want either for liquid or solid sustenance.

It is not an ancient place. It was founded in the early years of the nineteenth century by John Darcy of Kiltullagh, and it still bears the simple Georgian character of that period. Darcy had grand and patriarchal ideas and intended to be, as it were, the lord of the manor in more than name only – for instance, after the example of Martin of Ballynahinch, he included a jail for the better regulation of his tenants. Darcy's large stone house, his 'castle', still stands outside the town, on a stone-wall-patterned hillside falling to Clifden Bay, but it has long been empty and roofless.

The hills gather about Clifden and next to the town the land falls precipitately to the head of the bay, which at this point is narrow like a creek. From the steep hills above Darcy's castle there are fine views of the town punctuated by its two spires, views you are sure to find on postcards in the shops.

There is also a panorama of streams and bays and the indented coast, a panorama that suggests rewarding fishing. Indeed, Clifden enjoys a reputation as a centre for both fresh-water fishing and for sea fishing. If you are a fisherman you might well come to Clifden especially for a salmon, and might catch one too, with the pleasure of the scenery as a bonus.

In August or September Clifden spreads itself for the Connemara pony show. It is not simply a horse show, with emphasis on the hardy breed of ponies that has been evolved out of the tough conditions of the bogs and hills. Much more goes on. Bands play, and there are competitions and exhibitions of cookery and produce, and of home crafts such as knitting and the spinning and weaving of tweed. All this against a background of a medley of voices, among which there are subtle differences of accent of various parts of Iar-Chonnacht and Connemara, the very different voices of Americans and Englishmen and various others, and the sound of Irish of the hinterland and of the Aran Islands.

Clifden is proud of its Sky Road, a spectacular high route climbing above Darcy's castle and following the road looping round a long peninsula between Clifden Bay and Streamstown Bay. I join my voice to those of others who urge visitors not to miss this splendid route. It has memorable views of a beautiful and irregular coast shredded into islands and peninsulas, and looks downwards and outwards to Inishark and Inisbofin, delectable lands ringed with foam. Nearer at hand is the inshore Omey Island, where at every tide the sea retreats to leave a wide and level expanse of sand over which you may cross to the island dry-shod. It is so firm that horse-races are held on it.

Down there among the welter of islands lies Inishturbot, or Turbot Island, which in 1978 had the distinction of receiving a BBC television crew looking for ways of Irish life. The island has a few houses on it and a school, but the population has been declining for years. When an accident with a currach removed several of the men it seemed that the island economy had received a blow that would not allow it to survive, and evacuation to the mainland was talked of. The BBC's publicity brought several inquiries about the island and its precise location, which had not been made clear in the broadcast. The filming of the programme had been carried out in clear and sunny weather, and it seemed that for many listeners in England Inishturbot appeared a kind of convenient Arcady. And only half a mile from the mainland too! And not far from Clifden and its shops! The tragedy of the currach, in which several of the island men lost their lives, seemed almost irrelevant against the attractive beauty of Inishturbot and the clear sea in which it was set. But that sea was the Atlantic and summer did not always reign. Life, I am sure, could be, and usually was, much more grim and hard than appeared on the television screen.

Farther north, Inishturk lies in the ocean, and then comes Clare Island. Beyond are the peaks of Corraun, and to the left of that the mountainous cliffs of Achill Island tapering to the arête of Achill Head, blue in the distance. To the east, above the peaks and heads of the Twelve Bens, with their unmistakable outline, lies the wilderness of the Nephin Beg, which is more than 2000 feet high.

As we descended from the Sky Road to run along above the long and narrow inlet of Streamstown Bay the old walls of Doon castle stood across the water. Doon was an O Flaherty stronghold, one of those that so terrified the good merchants of Galway city.

Farmhouse accommodation

We had booked accommodation for several days at a farmhouse called Taobh a' Locha (beside the lake) at Streamstown north of Clifden. It turned out to be three miles north of Clifden on the Westport road, and was a building that had been extended on two floors to provide the accommodation of four bedrooms over a dining-room. This is frequently the case with farmhouse accommodation, and it provides quarters that are rather like a small hotel with farmhouse attached. Mrs. O Toole was a friendly woman who made us at home at once. We were the last of the house's complement to arrive.

We saw our fellow guests at dinner that evening, and found them an international group. There was a young Vietnamese of Chinese origin with a French wife who did not speak English – her husband's English was perfect.

There was an English couple from the Midlands, 'doing' the west and astonished by its unEnglishness. There was an American woman, with a son of about seventeen, who travelled through Ireland looking immaculate in a suit of tweed. And there was us. Dinner was grilled salmon and with it we had a bottle of white wine – many farmhouses are licensed for beer and wines.

As the evening had turned out wet and windy, Mrs. O Toole suggested we might like to use her guest sitting-room after dinner, and we were glad to accept. The Vietnamese said shyly that he had a bottle of whiskey and should he bring it down and Mrs. O Toole produced the necessary glasses. We talked, as tourists always do, of where we had been that day and whilst we had been in Ireland, and where we intended to go next day, and where we ought to go, the things we should not miss; and of course hotels and farmhouses. We agreed that the advantage of farmhouses, compared with large hotels, was not only that they were cheaper than hotels, but that they were more intimate, and they gave better opportunities of getting to know our fellow travellers and of learning more about the people among whom we travelled.

After the meeting broke up, about twelve, my wife and I were saying goodnight to Mrs. O Toole – a 'goodnight' that changed to a discussion on the making of soda-bread – when there was a knock at the front door close by my hand. There in the darkness, half-lighted by the lamp in the hall, stood a roughly dressed man with a streak of shining silver radiance hanging from his hand. A few words were exchanged, unfavourable on Mrs. O Toole's side, and the man retreated into the dark with his silver burden. 'You would never know where they got that salmon' she said. 'Anyway, I get mine from the boats at Cleggan quay, and pay less for it than those fellas charge.' We stayed shortly afterwards at a farmhouse near the foot of Nephin mountain, which rises like a great cone with a topping of quartz. It looks for all the world as though icing-sugar had been dredged over it. The farmhouse was not one that had been extended for visitors, but it was anyway a large, two-storey, double fronted house. The woman of the house willingly concocted a generous and very acceptable *ad hoc* dinner for us, though we had arrived unforgivably late. While this was being prepared we waited in the family's little-used but well furnished sitting room, and while I was admiring a polished shotgun hanging on the wall, the farmer, a young man, came in to welcome us. 'That thing is a sham', he said, 'only an ornament. If you would like to come shooting rabbits on the hill with me tomorrow morning I could lend you the real thing.' Such hospitality is not unusual in Ireland.

In the morning we had breakfast in a large room full of shiny, dark, heavy furniture, sitting at a massive and extensive table surrounded by chairs sufficient for a banquet.

We were joined at breakfast by a cheerful gentleman who turned out to be a millinery representative, a regular visitor to the house. He knew his job back to front and discoursed on its intricacies, and peculiarities in the Irish field, giving us an interesting insight into fashions in hats in Ireland, and in the great festivals of the Catholic church. We were glad to have met him and to add him to our collection of Irish characters.

The Sky Road rejoins the T71 north of Clifden and for a short distance this main road skirts the head of Streamstown Bay. as we continue northwards, with the bare elephantine contours of Mweelrea coming into view over the shoulders of Doughruagh and Altnagaighera, a sideroad goes off west to Cleggan, where currachs and other small boats and fishing-boats come in to a pleasant little harbour. From here the mail-boat takes passengers to Inishbofin. The name means 'the island of the white cow'. Inishbofin is inhabited and has a harbour, and is an excellent place for a quiet, withdrawn holiday, with fishing, sailing, and cliff-walking among its pleasures. Bishop Colman of Lindisfarne founded a monastery here in the seventh century, and a ruined church remains. Inishbofin – pronounce it 'Innish-bo-fin' – was, with Inishturk to the north and Clare Island beyond, which is part of the kingdom of Grace O Malley, or Granuaile, a termagant of a woman who, with numerous followers, fought and raided along the western coasts. She enjoys a reputation in Irish romantic legend altogether undeserved, but she was real enough, and bold. She visited Queen Elizabeth in England and is said to have claimed equality with that formidable lady. The contrast of the wild Irish female buccaneer with the bedizened and bejewelled Queen of England must have been piquant.

If the weather is good you may also go from Cleggan, or perhaps from

Inishbofin, in a currach if you choose, to visit High Island beyond the peninsula of Aughrus Point. St. Feichin founded a monastery here, with the usual penchant of Irish saints for islands remote and difficult of access. The remains of an early church and the monks' beehive huts or clocháns stand with a number of cross-incised slabs within an encircling wall or cashel.

We returned past Ballynakill and the inletted Ballynakill Harbour, against the background of the long, low Tully Mountain, to Dawros, where we turned left for Tully Cross. The Catholic church in this village has three windows in bright blue glass by Harry Clarke.

Holiday cottages

In the village is an example of the rent-a-cottage movement – nine especially designed and built thatched cottages for letting by the week to holiday-makers. Here a family may have the pleasure of independence, living in an Irish cottage with white walls and traditional half-door below thatch, in an Irish village, and enjoy a pleasant intimacy with the local people in pub or bar or in the shops from which their supplies will come. There are several places in the west and elsewhere where such holiday cottages have been built, as for example at Ballycastle in county Mayo – where a group of ten cottages forms a delightful village adjacent to the old village of Ballycastle. In such cottages you may go 'native' if you wish and cook in an iron corcán or a bastable hanging from iron pot-hooks over a turf fire – the means are available – but in case you find this tedious or difficult there is a modern gas-stove or electric stove. There is also electric lighting, modern sanitation, and a well-fitted bathroom.

The finance for these schemes comes partly from Bord Fáilte, partly from bank loans, and partly from participation by local people investing their capital. The motive power and direction may come in part from the parish priest – at Ballycastle we were shown around by a young and amiable nun, who was on the board of management.

Though they strive to maintain the Irish country character, with considerable success, the holiday cottages differ from the average country cottage in many respects. They are patently better designed (by architects), better crafted, better equipped and furnished, and usually larger. Many ordinary country cottages are very small – see an example in the main street of Ballycastle, and many of the cottages in Cois Fhairrge west of Spiddal, and of course anywhere in the west generally.

The holiday cottage might be said to represent what the better native Irish cottage might have become if Ireland, like England, had enjoyed a long period of peace and prosperity.

It is ironical that while holiday cottages are being built for the benefit of visitors, the Irish get out of their old cottages as soon as they can, and the government in many cases does its best to help them, regarding the native cottage as sub-standard housing. A new bungalow or new house standing next to an abandoned cottage is a common sight throughout Ireland. The forsaken cottage becomes a cowshed or a store, or is just left to fall down.

It will be a long time before the low, white-walled thatched cottage, beloved and romanticised by the painter Paul Henry and admired as quaint by innumerable tourists, disappears from the Irish scene, but clearly that is the direction in which things are going. In the meantime the visitor in holiday cottages such as those at Ballycastle and Tully Cross enjoys the advantages of modern living and modern housekeeping in an ambience approximating to traditional style.

West of Tully Cross, in Rinvyle, St. John Gogarty, a doctor and ebullient author of *As I was going down Sackville Street* and other books in the 'thirties, had a house. It was in the previous century the home of a branch of the Blake family, one of the tribes of Galway and therefore well known in the district. Mrs. Blake had some difference with the Land League and she opened the house as an hotel. Somerville and Ross stayed there during their tour of Connemara in a governess cart, and they described the house as old and full of panelled rooms containing medieval and Elizabethan furniture. The house has suffered one or two conflagrations since then, but it is again an hotel. There is a sandy strand near by, and beyond, near a headland that looks out to Inishbofin, stands a ruined castle of the O Flahertys. In the garden of a cottage is a dolmen, certainly a remarkable companion for a modern dwelling.

From the road in the region of the hamlet of Gowlaun east of Tully Cross there is a grandstand view of the mighty mass of Mweelrea mountain, which raises its 2688 feet directly from the sea and so has visually the full benefit of its height. It is not the highest mountain in Ireland, but such is its effect, so massive are its bare, folded slopes between sky and sea, that you might be forgiven for thinking that it should be. I have never climbed it, but it seems to me that Mweelrea, with Croagh Patrick, which I have climbed, is among the most attractive of the mountains of Connacht.

Kylemore

We return to Tully Cross and retrace our way to Letterfrack, a neat village, reflecting in its plain, efficient solidity its foundation in the nineteenth century by a Quaker. Behind it is Diamond Hill, which may have its name for all I know from the manner in which its slab-like slopes reflect the sky like the facets of a giant diamond. With Doughruagh to the north it forms a defile, in the bottom of which runs the salmon-inhabited Dawros river coming out of Pollnagcappul Loch and Kylemore Loch. The T71 accompanies the river and as you go along past blossoming rhododendrons you come suddenly to a view of Kylemore Abbey with its white limestone towers against the dark, steep, wooded slopes of Doughruagh, reflected in the surface of the lake at its door. You will surely have seen pictures of this abbey, but nonetheless you will scarcely restrain a gasp of amazement and of pleasure.

The abbey, a battlemented, neo-gothic castle, is dramatic in the extreme and deliberately picturesque. It might be a stage-set but for its evident solidity. If it is bogus and a pastiche of a distant day, or of something that never was, you will destroy a genuine delight if you give too free a rein to your critical faculties. The castle was built as a dwelling by a wealthy Liverpool merchant, Mitchell Henry, who conceived an extraordinary desire for a romantic castle in Ireland and had the money to make it a reality. He died in 1910. After the First World War the castle was taken over as a convent by the Benedictine Irish Dames of Ypres, a community of Catholic nuns who now returned to Ireland after many years abroad. They were a practical sisterhood. They opened the castle (which now became an 'abbey') as a guest-house. Later it was turned into a girls' school, which it still is. Visitors are welcome to enter the grounds, where there are a car-park and a souvenir shop. You may walk across the terrace in front of the abbey and continue through the woods beside the lake to a little church built for Henry in a rich and not unlearned fourteenth-century style, with charming stone-carving on doors and windows and, inside, shafts of Connemara marble.

The best time to visit the abbey is certainly in June or July when the fuchsia and rhododendrons are in bloom and the many trees planted by Henry and his successors are at their best.

There is a marvellous view of the abbey from the road near the beginning of Kylemore Loch, a view that would stop motorists in their tracks if the 'no-parking' signs could be ignored.

East of the abbey Kylemore Loch borders the road as the defile widens between the mountain of Garraun to the north and the outliers of the Twelve Bens to the south – Benbrack, in which the cold waters of the loch have their origin in the Kylemore river, and the lower Benbaun above the loch. The Maumturks loom ahead. Between the Maumturks and the Twelve Bens a minor but well surfaced road runs southwards in the valley, crossing the course of the Toureenacouna. A minor road, but it is one of the spectacles of Connemara, with the great sweeps of dun-coloured ground of the valley sloping up towards the steeper ascents of the mountains, which become an intense blue as the summits push towards the sky. In winter, when caps of white snow lie on the tops, the effect is astounding, as remote and cold as it is beautiful and attractive, as though it would draw one up there into the clear air and the invigorating ice. In the Maumturks, Letterbreckaun rises 2103 feet high above Loch Inagh, and in the Twelve Bens there are several summits near or exceeding 2000 feet – Benbaun and Bencollaghduff, Bencorr and Derryclare, Benbreen and Muckanaght. As you move along the road in the valley, beside the shore of Loch Inagh, these unchangeable mountains change their aspect, vary their slopes and colours. A great corrie, made in the ice ages and left hanging by a greater glacier flowing at right angles, opens high on the mountainside, and is succeeded as you pass by the blunt forehead of a sheer cliff. A scattering of hardy trees on the lower slopes serves to emphasise the heights of the mountains and the vastness of the scenery in which you are set. The moving, shining surface of Loch Inagh and of the succeeding Loch Derryclare accompany the road for miles and reflect the mountains with an impression of immense depths.

The valley is wild and lonely, so much so that you will be all the more surprised to come upon an occasional cottage, with a field or two painfully cultivated. (*Plate* 14.)

Below the emphatic eminence of Lissoughter and beside Loch Glendallough the road joins the T71 and we are once more on the route from Recess to Clifden. You have two choices. You may follow the main road once more to Clifden and on through Letterfrack to Kylemore and so repeat your steps and double your pleasure around the heartland of Connemara; or you may, as I have done, turn and go back up through the valley of the two lochs ('Glendalloch' means just that), Loch Derryclare and Loch Inagh, back to Kylemore. Such a return journey gives new views as of a different landscape and different mountains. So every memorable mile is memorable twice over.

Turning east on the main road to Leenaun (which is the T71 again), we find on an open moor, apparently far from any habitation that might provide a congregation, the extraordinary church of Our Lady of the Wayside. Its address is Creeragh, but where Creeragh may be is not evident. This modern church, whose four elevations are four triangles, compels passers-by to stop in amazement and to wonder what it can be doing here, just why, in fact the founder chose to set it down in this particular place. Certainly one may ask the same question of dozens of early churches whose ruins in lonely places or away on inaccessible islands are witness to the incorrigibility of saints; but the church of Our Lady must have been built to a different imperative, a motif that predicates the existence of a congregation. The puzzle may tempt you to come again on a Sunday or at some other time when a service of the mass is intended, to see just how a congregation materialises. I am assured that there are people within reach in the surrounding hills and glens, but how far the net must be cast is another matter. (*Plate* 20.)

The interior of the church is as interesting as the exclamatory elevations. The gable of the west window is occupied by a great and colourful Virgin Mary spreading her cloak above the worshippers. The subject naturally fills the triangle with which the glass-designer was presented. The furnishings are modern, with wrought iron for interesting and original stations of the Cross. Panels of stained glass enclose a baptistry.

The Killaries

A mile farther along the road we cross the Owenduff bridge and in yet another mile turn off west along a narrow road that shortly skirts the shore of Loch Fee, with the slopes of Garraun beyond. We are running parallel with Killary Harbour, which, unseen, is separated from us by a tongue of high land. Loch Fee is succeeded by Loch Muck, beside which the road divides, the left turn going back through Gowlaun to Tully Cross, the right to Salruck and Little Killary Bay. Salruck, a tiny place and far from anywhere, was one of those communities the world passed by and in which old customs and manners survived far into this century. A death, for example, was followed by a wake, that Irish custom that so fascinated Victorian commentators, who invariably thought it primitive and barbaric but, nevertheless, one of the colourful threads in the woof of Irish peasant life. The family and friends of the deceased would gather in the room where the body lay and women would weep and mourn over it and utter lamentations – 'keening' was the word for this. Porter and whiskey were served to the guests, and also clay pipes and tobacco, which the women might take as well as the men. A wake could go on for hours, or even all night, and a distinctly unsteady and bleary group would be left to accompany the coffin to the graveyard in the morning. At Salruck, as at some other places, the mourners took their pipes with them, and these were broken and the fragments were laid on the grave. There they could remain for many years. These pipe graveyards aroused frequent comment in the travel writings of the period. You may very likely never encounter a wake of the old kind in Ireland today, or hear of one, and you may fail to find a broken pipe on a grave at Salruck. Old customs die or are already dead.

A rough and narrow little road, with an occasional cottage, leads to the inlet of the Little Killary. It skirts the head of the inlet and runs beside a wall along the north shore. A few hardy trees ornament a pleasant but rocky landscape and are reflected in the water. They disappear as we go on and find ourselves in wilder country. The road ends at a small harbour, where you are likely to find two or three currachs in the water or turned upside down on the quay, where they are weighted down with stones to prevent the wind from blowing them away. They are used between March and August for netting salmon in the harbour and at other times for sea fishing and other purposes, including ferrying visitors to the foot of Mweelrea or along Killary Harbour. If you would like to undertake an excursion in one of these currachs inquire at any cottage for a boatman or at the Youth Hostel, the last building by the harbour. There is no fixed charge; you must strike a bargain with the boatman.

Many Youth Hostels are in strange places, and those who use them like it to be so, but nonetheless the situation of An Óige's hostel at Killary seems unexpected. But it has attractions that bring hostellers to occupy its 30 beds for men and 26 for women, despite the inconvenience of the nearest shop being six miles distant at Tully Cross and the nearest bus, once a day, five miles away. Having got here, making sure in advance that he has booked accommodation, the hosteller has the pleasure of the austere but beautiful scenery, with the great bulk of Mweelrea to the north, accessible by currach across the bay, the Killaries to the east, and the islanded sea to the west. And he may fish in the harbour or in the sea for a variety of fish, including bream, brill, mackerel, pollack, plaice, sole, turbot, and whiting, and with luck a sea-trout or a salmon; or he may haul up a splendid lobster.

It would be no wonder if you were reluctant to leave such a place, which I am sure could easily grow on you, to return alongside Loch Muck and Loch Fee to the T71. There we turn north and begin a descent towards the shore of the Killary, or to give it its name in full, Killary Harbour. Incidentally the pronunciation is '*Kill*-ary', with the accent on the first syllable. The name comes from 'caolaire', which means a narrow place; and this is exactly what the Killary is, a ten-mile narrow inlet of the sea, a veritable fiord, deep between steep mountains. It is accessible by road only along the shore of the inner end, along the T71 to Leenaun and Aasleagh. To explore the rest you must have a boat.

As you descend towards the Killary from the turning in the neighbourhood of Loch Fee, you have in front of you, apparently as vertical as a theatre drop, the long flank of Mweelrea, and then its 2303-foot neighbour Ben Gorm, the 'blue mountain'. Between them is a slot, the pass of the Bundorragha river – a name that means the 'dark end'. Soon you turn along the shore of the Killary, with only a wall between you and the water where the northern ends of the Maumturks dabble their toes, and come to Leenaun.

Leenaun is a sparse village strategically situated at a bend in the Killary, with a bridge over its tributary the Joyce river. There is a shop stocking, (as Irish country shops do), enough variety for a department store, with petrol pumps outside. There are an hotel, a terrace of houses, and some scattered bungalows,. Nothing that is remarkable or architecturally admirable. The two Killaries and the mountains make it a wonderful place. It is, as it were, the hub from which extend the Twelve Bens, the Mweelrea Mountains, and Ben Gorm, the Sheeffry Hills, the Partry Mountains rising in Devilsmother immediately above the village, the Joyce Country, and the Maumturk Mountains.

The main road follows the indentations of the shore of the Killary to the head of the inlet at Aasleagh, where the Erriff river comes down from the north-west to drop in a low but handsome waterfall that offers some compensation, when in spate, for the rain that is so likely to visit the mountainous country. It also provides an obstacle for the salmon to overcome on their way up the river to meet, perhaps, a fly on a line.

7
South County Mayo

At Aasleagh in Mayo the road goes through a little grove of trees, a rare thing in this country, and rhododendrons shine like coloured lamps beneath. Here you have a choice of alternative routes northward or north-eastwards, each of them attractive.

First you may go along the northern shore of Killary, treading on the toes of Ben Gorm, to the pass of the Bundorragha – put the accent on the *o* – Bun-*dorr* -haga. Here you turn sharply north with Mweelrea on your left and Ben Gorm on your right. The pass leads to Delphi. At Delphi there is nothing in particular – one of the lords of Sligo commemorated his experience of the Grand Tour by building a fishing lodge here and calling it by the name of the Greek oracle. No pythoness awaits at the Irish Delphi the expectant visitor inquiring after his future. All he will hear are the wind off the mountains, the lapping of lakes, and chuckling of the Owennagloch in the dark glen. And may be laughter of a salmon or a sea-trout at such foolishness.

In the glen a series of three lakes lie beside the road. Fin Loch, which means the bright or fair lake, Doo Loch, the dark or black lake, and Glencullin Loch, the loch of the holly tree glen. And in these fresh, cool mountain waters there are salmon – this I know because I have seen them on the end of a line. The fish come up into these lakes and streams from the Atlantic, between the islands of the sea and through the profundities of the Killary, to nose up the currents of the Bundorragha.

Beyond the lakes you may turn west along a minor road, passing a megalithic tomb conveniently situated by the roadside beneath a rocky bluff (and once supposed to be a holy well), to visit the seaward side of Mweelrea. A narrow road runs down between Mweelrea and the sea to the mouth of the Killary, where there is a broad, lonely, sandy strand. The mountain side rises on one hand and on the other you look over land falling to the sea and divided by a multitude of stone walls. Beyond are

Inishbofin and Inishturk, the island of the boar. In this country, among other interesting birds, you may see choughs, black birds distinguished by their red legs and red bills, a contrast with their sober suits – birds you may have seen last at O Brien's castle on Inisheer.

We go back through Killadoon, noticing the fine, long sandy strands, and Killeen, where a crowded graveyard includes a number of ancient cross-inscribed slabs among modern ones, a conjunction that suggests a continuing use for many centuries.

Louisburgh should have the s and the g pronounced, as though it were spelled 'Lewisburg'. It is a neat, plain, crossroads village a mile inland from Clew Bay. A minor road goes up and down over low hills to Roonah Quay, where you will see currachs and boats that will take you to Clare Island. Clare Island, once the headquarters of Grace O Malley, stands in the mouth of Clew Bay, a colourful jewel in the morning light, a black coal in the fire of the western sun. On the island there are remains of a thirteenth-century Cistercian abbey and of a sixteenth-century castle, said to have been Grace O Malley's. To the west on Clare Island the land rises to 1520 feet and falls in high cliffs to the sea. A long wall dividing the farm land from the mountain waste is visible from Roonagh Quay.

Croagh Patrick

East of Louisburgh and seen from far around rises Croagh Patrick, among the most graceful of mountains. St. Patrick is believed to have spent forty days and forty nights in prayer on the summit, and so the mountain is accounted holy and is the object of a great pilgrimage or pattern on Garland Sunday, the last Sunday in July. The mountain is of quartzite, and quartzite breaks up into sharp-edged stones or scree that is never rounded by the weather. This is the material the pilgrims walk over from Murrisk by the sea-shore to the *cruach* at the summit, where there is a small modern chapel, 2510 feet of hard slog. I have done it in stout shoes, but to make the pilgrimage all the more rewarding to their souls many of the pilgrims, especially women, do the climb in bare feet. Thousands of them trudge up the mountainside from the crack of dawn, in hot sun or in howling gale. If he were not too accustomed to it, God would be amazed by this devotion. However, if the climb is worth doing for the benefit of your soul, it is also worth doing for the admiration of God's good earth, for the beauty of the mountain and the magnificence of the view. Clew Bay lies below, its inner waters a clutter of half-drowned drumlins, the little, egg-shaped hillocks that are a result of a frolic of the glaciers during the ice ages. The maze of channels between the half-eroded, tear-drop islands must require local knowledge for its negotiation, but when seen from the heights of Croagh Patrick or the opposing Corraun the islands are very spectacular. The flow of drumlins may be traced inland for a long distance and in the waters of Clew Bay it makes a fairy world that reaches out towards the beauties of Clare Island. (*Plate* 13.)

Murrisk is the name given to the district south from Clew Bay and inland to Mweelrea and the Erriff river; it was one of the baronies of ancient Ireland. In particular the name denotes the few houses and the pub facing the bay at the foot of Croagh Patrick. The pub is the recognised beginning of the climb up the mountain. Here pilgrims may, and do, refresh themselves against the prospect of the feat and afterwards to overcome the exhaustion of its achievement.

Between the pub and the sea stand the ruins of an Augustinian friary founded in 1475, its battlemented walls rising directly from the shore. A cell was restored in 1942 and mass is again said here.

Westport and Newport

The main road, the T39, leads to Westport Quay and to Westport. Westport, a seigneurial town planned by James Wyatt for the Marquess of Sligo, clusters round its Octagon, in the centre of which is a plinth that once held a statue. A much prettier part is the Mall, along the middle of which runs a clear, purling stream sheltered by an avenue of trees. Canon Hannay, better known as the author George A. Birmingham, was incumbent of the ornate Protestant church.

Westport Quay was intended as the commercial outlet for the town and warehouses were built for the trade that was expected. It never came, and the solid stone warehouses remained empty.

Fishermen come to the quay now to join boats that will take them out to sea to fish for big game. Sharks are caught out in deep water and one day we saw a huge ray brought in. It was hauled up and spreadeagled on a gantry on the quayside, quite dead, and was left there for several days for the flies and the wasps.

The Marquess of Sligo's Westport House was designed in 1730 by the German architect Richard Cassels and altered fifty years later by James Wyatt. The result is a fine mansion that is well worth a visit – it is open to the public. In the park is a small zoo.

The alternative route to Westport from Aasleagh Falls follows along the valley of the Erriff river, which provides the water for the falls. The valley runs between the Partry Mountains on the east and the Sheeffry Hills on the west. The river is a popular salmon and sea-trout water, and by reason of that is commercialised, with organised beats marked by numbers on poles. You would have to book in advance to secure a favoured beat.

At Srahlea bridge the Erriff receives the Owenmore with the waters off Croagh Patrick. About three miles farther north a side-road goes off north-east to Aghagower, where, tradition says, St. Patrick founded a church. A monastery followed and in the period of the Norse raids this acquired a round tower, which is still there, restored. A thirteenth- or fourteenth-century church, now a ruin, remains on St. Patrick's site.

Westport is four and three quarters miles north-west.

North of Westport the road runs through the flow of green drumlins, which now, from ground level, appear as small hills, to Newport. Here at Newport there are parallel bridges. One of these bridges once carried a railway, which ran as far as Achill. Raised high at one end of the former rail bridge stands an impressive romanesque church, built in 1914 of roseate stone. It contains beautiful east windows by Harry Clarke, a burst of brilliant and exclamatory colour in the dim interior. Facing the church on the other side of the Newport river is an unusually large court for the Irish game of handball. The game is similar to squash and equally fast and furious, but it is played with the bare hand or fist. Simpler handball courts – three walls, with the back wall higher than the side walls – are found in many villages throughout the country.

Newport is a centre for sea fishing and for lake and river fishing and for the exploration of the vast mass of wild country centering on the 2065 feet of Nephin Beg. This area is penetrated by only one road, the road running up beside Loch Furnace and Loch Feagh to Srahmore. There at Srahmore – and it will be a surprise – you will find a simple little modern church with interesting glass and stations of the Cross. The two lochs are used for the scientific investigation of salmon breeding. The road is a dead end, or rather, continues only as a rough track into the mountains.

Rockfleet castle, or Carraigahooley castle, stands on slabby rock with its feet in the sea, a complete tower-house lacking only a bawn. The key is available locally. The tower was built by the Burkes and passed to

Grace O Malley by means of a notorious trick. She married Richard Burke on the understanding that the marriage might be terminated after a year by a simple declaration. She used the year to garrison the castle with her own men and kept it when, as she had probably intended from the beginning, she declared the marriage ended.

Farther on, beside Clew Bay, pleasantly situated beside an inlet, you will find Burrishoole abbey, a Dominican friary founded in 1469 by Richard Burke. The church is roofless, but is otherwise well preserved, and some of the domestic buildings still stand.

Mallaranny, on the narrow neck of land that connects with the Corraun peninsula, is a simple but pleasant village with an enormous sandy strand on the margin of Clew Bay. In the mild climate fuchsia, rhododendrons, and Mediterranean heath flourish and flower freely. Cleggan mountain, 1256 feet, gives good views of the landscape and the fragmented seascape of the bay.

Achill

Corraun is a great knob of land, reaching 1784 feet high, attached to the mainland by the isthmus of Mallaranny, and to Achill Island, over the long and narrow Achill Sound, by a bridge. Roads go north and south round Corraun to Achill, a complete ring along the coast. The more interesting road runs along the south coast, high above rocky coves in wild country beside Clew Bay. It turns north alongside Achill Sound, and you have views of Achill with its sparse cottages and the slender tower of Kildavnet castle. (*Plate* 23.)

The bridge crosses to the village of Achill Sound, where banks of rhododendrons provide a colourful contrast to the rest of this bleak island. Achill, in outline resembling an inverted letter L and measuring 57 square miles, is the largest of the islands off the coast of Ireland. It is mountainous and stony, with huge cliffs falling to the sea at Menawn, at Slievemore, and along the broken edge of Croaghaun at the western tip of the island. Splendid beaches lie along the coast, as for example, the vast expanse of Keel and the remote little bay of Keem.

The best introduction to Achill is enjoyed by following the Atlantic Drive. Take the road south from the village of Achill Sound, with its views of Corraun peninsula across the water. Near Kildavnet there is a small, ruined, early church beside the road. Kildavnet castle stands a little farther on. Popularly supposed to have been one of the castles of Grace O Malley, this slender tower, in outline largely complete, can

have been little more than a watchtower, for the interior measures only
about 8 feet by 12 feet. The second floor and the roof must have been
reached by ladder, for there would have been no room for stairs. The
castle stands picturesquely beside the shore, and with a boat or two
drawn up to the little quay, beside the weedy rocks, it makes a popular
subject for pencil or camera.

The road follows the line of the south tip of the island, and there offshore
is the island of Achill Beag. The route now runs north, winding high on
the sides of cliffs, and swoops vertiginously down beside a sheer fall
edged by a curb of white stones, to pass an inlet or a little bay. Notices
warn caravanners of the very evident dangers – notices addressed
primarily to horse-caravanners – the popularity of the tinker type of
caravan for holidays brings holidaymakers to some hair-raising
adventures. The Atlantic Drive requires extreme caution from the
drivers of horse-drawn caravans, and equally from the drivers of cars. I
would not recommend it for trailer caravans.

The road eventually brings you to the village of Keel, with the
fantastic Cathedral Rocks of the Menaun cliffs rising beyond the
expansive sandy beach. Keel is one of the principal villages of Achill. Its
whitewashed houses group nicely at the west end of the bay, and a little
farther west is Dooagh. These, like other villages on Achill, once remote,
country places, with the inhabitants gaining a precarious living, are now
holiday centres, without losing their island quality. The narrow road
climbs steadily to a high viewpoint looking steeply down on Keem Bay
at the head of a sound and backed by a hill that thins out to the
incredibly narrow promontory of Achill Head, a knife-edge ridge or
arête in the ocean. You may return from Dooagh by the northern road
along the foot of Slievemore, where deserted upland cottages recall the
old custom of 'booleying' or transhumance – the move to summer
pastures on the mountain, with the people living in temporary booley
houses – what in Scotland are called 'shielings'. There is also a deserted
village, its empty and roofless houses mute yet eloquent of the life that
once went on here. At the village of Doogort you touch the sea again on
your way back to Achill Sound.

In the spring and early summer basking-shark, measuring up to 35
feet in length, come into Achill waters and are hunted by the islanders.
The method is to surround the shark with a net as it lies basking on the
surface and to kill it with harpoons thrown from a small boat, which may
be a currach. The fish is principally useful for its liver, which yields a

large quantity of oil, an oil that was once the fuel of the cottage lamps. The best place to see fishing for basking-shark is Keem Bay.

The presence of sharks of these massive dimensions near the island shores may seem alarming, but nervous visitors need not be concerned about these monsters – they seldom come inshore, and in any case their throats are too small to swallow a bather. Their food is plankton, not human flesh.

Belmullet and the Mullet

North of Mallaranny the T71 runs over a vast bog, a queer place, in its way as wild as the mountainous country of the Nephin Beg upland to the east of the road. The bog is a rich source of turf and its levels are cut mechanically to supply a power station.

Bangor Erris is a small place with a prominent quarry beside the clear and stony Owenmore river – 'Erris' is the name of this whole district of north-west Mayo, one of the ancient baronies. It includes the sea-scalloped peninsula of the Mullet. Bangor is called 'the gateway of Erris', but just a little to the north-west is a narrow gap more easily defended – and it *was* once defended, for on a low hill no bigger than a motte, beside the road and a little stream, stands the ruin of the ancient fort of Dún Domnaill.

Beyond the extensive Carrowmore Lake the T58 goes on to Belmullet, perhaps the loneliest town in Ireland, on a slender isthmus just wide enough to prevent the Mullet from being an island. The Mullet is a remote and exiguous peninsula, about fifteen miles long, with its shores on the east side, facing Blacksod Bay, scooped into enormous curves that come near to dividing the peninsula into a chain of islands. On the west side it faces the turbulent seas of the Atlantic. There are a few sparse villages and many good sandy beaches and bays, and excellent fishing, but few strangers or tourists come to the Mullet, and this is certainly their loss. From the scattered village of Fallmore at the southern end there are views of the hills and the mighty cliffs of Achill, to the east rise the summits of the Nephin Beg, and to the west, out in the wild Atlantic, there lie the islands of Inishglora and the North and the South Inishkeas, which, being difficult of access, were inevitably chosen by monks and hermits as desirable places to found cells and monasteries.

Inishglora, the 'island of the voice', lies offshore from Cross Abbey, which may be reached to within half a mile by car from Bellmullet. Cross Abbey is a medieval church, standing on the site of a sixth-century foundation of St. Brendan's. The present Cross Abbey is set in a graveyard in which there have been so many burials through the centuries that the earth within the encircling wall has risen to its level. The place is still holy, as is the case with most ancient Irish churchyards, and the gravestones, old and recent, jostle together and lean at various angles against the strong winds from the ocean.

The land here drops to the sea in sheer cliffs, and out there in a welter of foam Inishglora lies in the sea, with another monastery founded by St. Brendan. The remains are much older than what is to be seen at Cross and may be as old, at least in part, as the time of St. Brendan, which would be the mid sixth century. The monastery is of the Celtic type, with two churches within the usual encircling wall, and a third church outside – St. Brendan's Oratory and the Saints' Church (which is mortared) inside the wall and Teampall na mBan – the Women's Church or the Nuns' Church – outside. There are ancient cross slabs and there is a holy well reached by seven descending steps.

Inishglora marked the end of one of the ancient legends of Ireland, a legend not very well known in England.

Lír, a king of ancient times – from whom, incidentally, Shakespeare's Lear is derived – had three children, two boys and a girl called Fionnuala. Lír, a widower, married a second time. Aoife, Lír's new wife, grew jealous of her stepchildren, and by her enchantments turned them into swans, condemned to swim on the waters and seas of Ireland through many centuries. They were to be released by the sound of St. Patrick's bell proclaiming the advent of the Christian gospel. Thus they quartered the seas, from the Moyle, which is the channel between Ireland and Scotland, round to the cold Atlantic and down the west coast. Immortal as swans, they dreamed of the day when they should regain their human form as the children of Lír, but their stepmother's enchantment was more wicked than they knew. When Patrick's bell was heard the swans were off the coast of Inishglora, and they came ashore with joy, their great black feet cleaving through the surf, expecting their avian shape to be transformed in a flash. And so it was. But they had lived for centuries as swans and the years remained. The children of Lír were old and decrepit and they died at once of sheer senility.

Thomas Moore wrote one of his Irish melodies about it, called 'The Song of Fionnuala', which, with that marvellous facility he possessed, he made to sing memorably:

Silent, O Moyle, be the roar of thy water,
  Break not, ye breezes, your chain of repose,
While, murmuring mournfully, Lír's lonely daughter
  Tells to the night-star her tale of woes.
When shall the swan, her death-note singing,
  Sleep with wings in darkness furled?
When will heaven, its sweet bell ringing,
  call my spirit from this stormy world?

Sadly, O Moyle to thy winter wave weeping,
  Fate bids me languish long ages away;
Yet still in her darkness doth Erin lie sleeping,
  Still doth the pure light of dawning delay.
When will that day-star, mildly springing,
  Warm our isle with peace and love?
When will heaven, its sweet bell ringing,
  Call my spirit to the fields above?

The first four lines are the best and most memorable. After that, and especially in the second stanza, one is not quite sure whether Moore is writing of Fionnuala or of the political state of Ireland in his own day. Moore often played the part of the singer of Irish patriotism, and the English, perhaps not recognising the politics in his ditties, loved him for it. Yet Moore might easily have been hanged with Robert Emmett. The leader of the rebellion of 1798 – and Moore's friend – deliberately kept Moore clear of embroilment in it.

Farther south are the North and South Inishkeas, which were inhabited until 1937 – many of the islands of the west, from Inishkea down to the Blaskets off the coast of Kerry, have given up their populations in modern times, because the fishing has declined perhaps or life has become harder, or for some other reason. The monks and hermits of early Christian times, however, chose such places for preference. North Inishkea, for example, bore a flourishing monastery, of which the most obvious remnant is a large mound, 500 feet across and 60 feet high, bearing beehive huts and the remains of square houses. This is called An Baile Mór, the big town.

A quantity of purpura shells was discovered in the monastery. Purpura is the shell fish from which the ancients produced the famous Tyrian purple. The shell fish were probably used on Inishkea for making an ink or paint for the painting and writing of manuscripts, and we may imagine the monks of Inishkea sitting in their narrow cells, within the ambiance and the sound of the sea, with the sea-birds crying above them, sharpening their quills and pointing their brushes to produce pages of vellum bearing letters and images of marvellous beauty. They had all the time in the world and they could pause to gaze out through the doorway to watch the crashing of the waves and the rising of the spray beyond the rocks of the foreground. Perhaps they might dream or compose a little poem as a gloss in the margin of the leaf they were writing. It could have been in such a monastery in such circumstances that a monk idly sat admiring his white cat and wrote the original Gaelic of the following poem:

> *I and Pangur Bán my cat,*
> *'Tis a like task we are at;*
> *Hunting mice is his delight,*
> *Hunting words I sit all night.*
>
> *Better far than praise of men*
> *'Tis to sit with book and pen;*
> *Pangur bears me no ill will,*
> *He too plies his simple skill.*
>
> *'Tis a merry thing to see*
> *At our tasks how glad are we,*
> *When at home we sit and find*
> *Entertainment to our mind.*
>
> *Oftentimes a mouse will stray*
> *In the hero Pangur's way:*
> *Oftentimes a keen thought set*
> *Takes a meaning in its net.*
>
> *'Gainst the wall he sets his eye*
> *Full and fierce and sharp and sly;*
> *'Gainst the wall of knowledge I*
> *All my little wisdom try.*
>
> *When a mouse darts from its den,*
> *O how glad is Pangur then!*
> *O what gladness do I prove*
> *When I solve the doubts I love!*

So in peace our tasks we ply
Pangur Bán, my cat, and I;
In our arts we find our bliss,
I have mine and he has his.

Practice every day has made
Pangur perfect in his trade;
I get wisdom day and night,
Turning darkness into light.

This English version, one of several translations that have been made by various persons, is by Robin Flower.

You may get to Inishglora or the Inishkeas and sample the solitude of the islands, with nothing to disturb you but sheep – and you are likely to disturb them more than they you – but you may not find it as straightforward as a Sunday excursion. There is no regular boat service. You should ask at a cottage for the whereabouts of a boatman, and when you have found one you must fix a price with him and put yourself in his hands. The weather may delay your visit for a day or two.

We walked over the rough, tussocky grass where cattle stood with their flanks steaming in the cool sea air, back to the car and drove south over roads scattered with quantities of wind-blown sand down to Fallmore. The houses of the village stand far apart as though they were so many smallholdings rather than a coherent village and they may be seen scattered across the landscape in a spectacular view from a rise in the road. The view looks out over the houses to the islanded sea and Blacksod Bay, and beyond to Achill and its great cliffs grey above the water. Nearer at hand stands the island of Duvillaun Mór (big black island) – uninhabited and accessible only in calm weather – if you want to go there one of the local farmers, who are also fishermen, could be persuaded to take you. Fifty or sixty years ago a small community of hardy islanders eked out a living on Duvillaun Mór and the remains of their village still stand, with seabirds calling over its deserted gables and emphasising its abandonment and isolation. Many generations before them a few monks toiled in unresponsive fields and said their masses in a primitive monastery, where a slab bearing a carved Crucifixion shows evidence of their piety.

To the west the emphatic Blacksod Rock is topped by a lighthouse. Neighbouring villages near Fallmore have the curious names of

Search View and Glosh. The former is obviously English in origin, while the second sounds as though it might be derived from a Gaelic word, *glas* or *glais* which might mean a stream or a verdant place.

I wonder if the name of Search View comes from the near-by apparent castle, guarding the coast with bartizans and battlements, which was someone's romantic notion of what a coastguard tower or a signal tower ought to look like.

Near Fallmore stands an early, and now of course ruined church dedicated to a little-known saint called Derivla. The church may date from the seventh century, but there were later alterations, including the carved decoration of the round-headed doorway, which is probably twelfth century. 'Derivla' is a feminine name and it suggests that here on the far end of the Mullet, as far from interruption as they could get without going into the sea to Duvillaun or the Inishkeas, there was a small community of nuns. It endured at least five centuries, and perhaps, with that notable persistence of Irish religious houses, it was still active at the Reformation and beyond, a thousand years after its foundation.

All the commerce of the Mullet is channelled through the town of Belmullet. Indeed, it cannot go any other way, for the town stands like a sentinel on the isthmus that is all that prevents the Mullet from being an island. This isthmus attaches it to the mainland – but a lonely and remote part of the mainland here in the far north-west corner of Mayo, the barony of Erris. There is a regular market, lining the main street above the stone pier, where a variety of new and second-hand clothing is sold and you may buy anything from agricultural tools to fish fresh from the sea. On market days there seem to be more people in Belmullet than you would suppose could possibly live in the district round about.

8
North County Mayo

To the north the cliffs of Erris Head form one of the bulwarks of the inlet of Broad Haven, along the southern shore of which the T58 connects Bellmullet with Bangor Erris. A surfaced side-road goes north to Portacloy, passing the fishing hamlet of Pollathomish on Sruwaddacon Bay, a profound sea cleft with cliffs enclosing sandy strands. A double, concentric stone circle is ascribed to the druids, in default of anyone more likely in popular estimation.

The narrow up and down country road to Portacloy drops down to the village at the head of Portacloy Bay, a constricted inlet between the cliffs of Benwee Head and Doomara. From Portacloy you can follow a footpath over rugged but admirable country to a height of over 800 feet at Benwee Head itself, where the land abruptly comes to an end by plunging the whole of that distance into the sea. Out in the water, two miles away, rise the Stags of Broadhaven, triangular rocky islets set in permanent rings of foam and apparently totally inaccessible to other than seabirds. You may see them from the partial shelter of a small coastguard lookout on Benwee Head, now windowless and floored with sheeps' droppings. The former occupants kept themselves warm with a small fireplace fed with turf they skimmed from the mountain-side, as you may see.

To the west you will see the cliffs of Erris Head, the most northerly projection of the Mullet, beyond the wide mouth of Broadhaven.

To the east, lies a series of gigantic cliffs and far beyond that, grey-blue in the depths of the atmosphere, the mountains of Sligo.

Some people like to tramp along the cliff-tops between Benwee and Belderg or Downpatrick Head, and it is certainly invigorating and testing country, with cliffscape after cliffscape providing splendid views and not a little peril for the unwary or the overadventurous. For their benefit a Youth Hostel was set up at Pollathomish.

If you wish to continue eastwards by car you will have to return from Portacloy, leaving its remote, sandy beach – which, probably, you have had to share only with natives of the district busy about their daily work – to go some miles inland towards Loch Carrowmore. There you may join a narrow country road leading to Belderg. Here the little Belderg river contains salmon and consequently you may encounter ardent fishermen ambitious to capture one of those delectable fish. To the north there is a small harbour with a stony foreshore on which we found several currachs. Even on this kind of shore these simple boats of lath and tarred canvas are serviceable, as they have been in Ireland for who can say how many centuries.

Belderg and Downpatrick Head

The cliffs at Belderg harbour and the stones of the strand are composed of a hard, dark rock glittering with spangles of mica (*Plate* 19).

If you are not tempted by the walk along the cliffs from Portacloy to Belderg – and, believe me, it is very rough country – you could consider it worth while to view the cliffs from a boat. You might hire a boat and crew at Belderg, or you might do it at the inset, delightful little harbour of Portacloy. And if you hire a boat for this purpose why not let it be a currach and emulate St. Brendan at least for a little distance? The cliffs are magnificent seen from the sea, with their sheer precipices plunging down to a foamy ocean. The most impressive is the Hill of Glinsk, which is over 1000 feet high and seems to fall all that distance. Below it is Moista Sound, a narrow chasm of the sea between vertical cliff faces.

To the east the road comes near the sea and descends to the ravine of the Glenglossara river, where banks of rhododendrons appear unexpectedly exotic in this stony landscape. Above Benaderreen Bay the road looks forward towards Downpatrick Head, with its colourful horizontal strata and its chopped-off island of Doonbristy.

Glance inland to the south of the bay and you may glimpse an unusually tall and slender standing stone. This is in the graveyard of Doonfeny. This stone, eighteen feet high and only about nine inches through, rises on a little mound in a cluster of gravestones of various periods, in a graveyard that has evidently been revered for many hundreds of years. It was so evidently when some now unknown holy man erected the stone and a church to mark his coming there and the proclamation of Christianity. A cross carved on one face of the stone confirms it as a Christian monument. There is more than one tall stone in Ireland that is called the tallest in the country, and this one may well deserve the superlative.

Holy places abound in Ireland and some of them are very beautiful and some are spectacular, some in deep glens and some high in the air, as is the summit of Croagh Patrick. Many of them of all kinds bear the name of St. Patrick, who appears to have been a very peripatetic gentleman, even in that time, when the essence of sainthood was travel in whatever vehicle came handy. It was nothing for a saint to cross the sea in a sieve or conversely floating on a mill-stone. Old stories to explain natural features will draw you to Downpatrick Head, which, as the name tells you, was a resort of St. Patrick. The head forms the eastern side of the rocky Buntrahir Bay – rocky but it has half a mile of sand as clean and attractive as you could wish, with a fresh and invigorating sea beating translucently on the strand. But you will not be here very long before curiosity draws you to inspect the wonders of this headland and its curious island of Doonbristy.

Clambering from the strand you walk over springy, sheep-bitten, salty turf and soon find the ruins of an early church, a holy well, and a statue of St. Patrick. St. Patrick was here, so they say, and in commemoration of his visit an annual pilgrimage or 'pattern' takes place on Garland Sunday. 'Patterns', I am told, are not what they were in the old days – the old days being, I would guess, before the First World War; nowadays the young do not observe them as their elders did.

That may be so, but what in any case was St. Patrick doing here apart from casting the snakes out of the country and proselytising its inhabitants? He was having a mighty row, that is what he was doing, a veritable battle, with a wicked landlord, say some, but perhaps with the incarnation of the devil – which he must have been to deserve the extremities to which the saint was driven. The two opponents struggled with each other mightily and in their thrashing about they knocked a bit of the headland off into the sea – and that must be true, for the tall, islanded stack of Doonbristy is the proof of it. (*Plate* 15.)

In the end Patrick caught his opponent a whack over the head with his crozier, and so mighty was his arm and so hefty his crozier that he hammered the fellow down like a peg, down through the rock of the headland and clean through the roof of a sea-cave that was below.

The cave, a great puffing-hole plangent with the noise of the sea, is there still for anyone to see. If you look down into its depths you might see a seal or two sheltering there from the wind and the rush of the tide.

The puffing-hole is called 'Pollnashantinny', which is good Gaelic but of uncertain meaning. It might be 'Poll na sean tuine', meaning 'the hollow of the old woman', or it could be 'Poll na sean teine', which would mean 'the hollow of the old fire'. Neither seems relevant – unless Patrick's opponent really was the flaming devil!

Origins in ancient legends might seem difficult to surpass, but a glance into the probable geology of Pollnashantinny suggest something that is also exciting. The sea, driving into the softer rock, eroded a long, blind tunnel, and the tide continued there, busily thrusting and sucking. When the sea was strong it must have worked with enormous force, compressing and driving a ram of air into the space at the end of the tunnel, with a great roaring noise that would have been heard and felt above ground on the headland – if there was anyone there to hear. At last the pressure would have been too great for the eroded rock and it may have given way suddenly with an explosion like a bomb and fragments of rock flying up into the air.

The other piece of wreckage I have mentioned as a result of St. Patrick's fracas is Doonbristy, a tall column of horizontal strata multicoloured like layer-cake. It has a cap of ragged turf, among the tufts of which lie the stones of a prehistoric promontory fort built two or three thousand years ago when the island and the mainland were still joined. The stack is too far distant from the mainland for anyone to think of getting there other than by helicopter – unless you can cadge a lift from one of the gulls circling above the inimical waves.

The marvellous cliffs, with their horizontal and variegated strata, like those of Doonbristy, as ragged and brittle as slates, entering and re-entering the headland in curving lines, form long sheltered ledges that are ideal for the seabirds. And the seabirds cling here by the thousand, or the tens of thousands, now and then to launch themselves and fly a circle or two, shrilly calling across the voids above the sea, before they swing in to their perch once more. I lay on the nibbled grass above the cliff edge and looked at the birds through binoculars. Terns, jaunty and elegant, with their pointed beaks distinguishing them from gulls; gulls of several kinds and several sizes, with crueller, yellow beaks and grey and darker plumage of several species; skuas, which are highway-men, stealing their food from others; razorbills and guillemots, and the clown-faced puffins, their beaks like striped humbugs, all took part in the perpetual dance and brouhaha of the cliff faces. I clapped my hands and a great cloud of birds rose from their perches and swung round, shouting and protesting, and, then, wheeling and planing, they returned to their places, and for all I know each may have had his own particular nook.

Ballycastle cottages

Ballycastle, to the south-east, is a small place, with its buildings, including those of the older kind of thatched cottages, pouring down an inclined street with its two facing churches, Protestant and Catholic, like a brood with two hens. There are ten or eleven pubs, in almost any one of which you can drink and listen to ballad-singing. And that was all you needed to know about Ballycastle in Mayo until a few years ago. Then the village entered the holiday cottage movement and, aided by the banks and by Bord Fáilte, the priests and the nuns, and by practically anybody who could put up a pound or two for a share in the enterprise, the necessary capital was got together and a distinctive village of holiday cottages was begun. There was plenty of expert advice, and – in the result, I may add – able architects, and a group of ten holiday cottages rose in a field just outside the old village.

We knew nothing of this and we came upon the holiday village with surprise as we walked down across the fields from Lacken Bay, seeing it at a distance. It was neat and bright, with its new stone walls and its new thatched and tiled roofs.

It was surprising because you never saw such cottages in the district before. At first glance they appeared English, like something out of Somerset or Sussex, but another glance shows the Irish characteristics. But yet they were unlike the old Irish cottage – compare, for example, the cottages in the street of the old village. The new ones are larger and better designed.

You may live as approximately as you wish in the old country style, cooking over a turf fire in corcáns and bastables – the iron vessels of the old cottager, hung from the iron hook in the hearth, such as used to be part of the furniture of every cottage – but I daresay you will soon get tired of that. When you do there are all the implements and facilities of the modern housewife close at hand – gas or electric cookers, electric lighting, showers, and heating – and if you wish for services for cooking, washing-up, and bed-making I am sure you could be accommodated.

The cottages will sleep five to eight persons and the cost varies with the time of year.

The hand-made quilts, the simple furniture, and the primitive cooking, with the scent of burning turf may seduce you to a simpler way of life than you are accustomed to – with the knowledge that you may at any moment renege on your resolutions and return to modern domestic facilities. But there is one thing that you will not find that was once part of the common furniture of an Irish cottage. This was a spinning-wheel. In old photographs a spinning-wheel may sometimes be seen, with the woman of the house sitting beside in her long, full skirt – the skirt always seemed to be black. Black, however, was how the photographic emulsion of those days rendered madder red, the common colour of the countrywoman's skirt in the west.

Irish spinning-wheels might be very utilitarian devices, possibly made at home with the assistance of the local joiner and blacksmith. One such wheel was photographed by J.M. Synge, the playwright, on Aran. The photograph appears as plate 33 of the collection of Synge's pictures arranged by Lilo Stephens under the title *My Wallet of Photographs*.

North of Ballycastle lies Lacken Bay, a shallow inlet in which in the inner part at least, the tide spreads as no more than a film of water, and towards its close not even that. Here in the spring an abundant cover of thrift spreads a sheet of pink blossom thickly over the sand, from the sand-dunes that rim the strand out to the lapping margin of the sea.

Killala and Ballina

In the next opening to the east, Killala Bay, in 1794, three frigates bearing English colours dropped anchor. The two sons of the Bishop of Killala, anxious to see aboard an English warship, took a boat and rowed out to the frigates. They were welcomed aboard and promptly made prisoner. The frigates, the boys discovered, were French, carrying 1500 men of the French army, veterans of the Rhine and of the campaign in Italy, under the command of General Humbert. The expedition had come to assist the Irish to set up a republic, in the full expectation of finding a people ready and anxious to rise with them. Humbert had brought arms and uniforms for many men, but he had brought little money. When he entered Killala he was constrained to issue assignats in exchange for supplies, assignats that might (or might not) be cashable in the future on the directory of Connacht, which would be set up when that province was secured.

Humbert advanced from Killala to Ballina, which he took without difficulty, the English forces not having fully recovered their senses, and pushed on to Castlebar. There the English were waiting for him on the bridge and a battle ensued. Humbert won this encounter, the English fleeing so precipitately that the battle has ever since been known in Irish history as 'the races of Castlebar'.

Humbert stayed in Castlebar for a few days, but he must already have known that his situation was hopeless. His three ships, not wishing to be caught by the British fleet, had returned to France and his expedition was marooned in a country that could offer him little assistance or reinforcement. Certainly he received recruits, but for the most part they were untried countryman and were not numerous. On the 4th September he drew out of Castlebar and set his face towards Sligo. Harried by the British he moved on to Dromahair, where he threw five of his guns over the bridge into the river. The British pursued him with caution, avoiding another bloody nose, but at Ballynamuck the French turned and surrendered.

Yeats places the events of his play *Cathleen ní Houlihan* in a cottage inland from Killala Bay on the day the French landed. Cathleen is a personification of Ireland who calls a young man away from his sweetheart to defend his country.

On his way to Killala Humbert would have passed the ruins of Rathfran abbey, but would probably not have taken much notice of it unless it were useful for concealing or billeting troops. It was just another of the numerous monastic ruins of the countryside.

Rathfran abbey was in fact a friary, founded for Dominicans in 1274. Parts of it were rebuilt in the fifteenth and sixteenth centuries, but the long, narrow church with its lancet east window, is probably of the original build. The living quarters and the cloisters, remains of which may be seen, are of the later structure. The friary was granted to Thomas Essex in 1577, and was set alight by the reprehensible Bingham, President of Connacht, in 1590; but the friars carried on their work in the district for another century or so.

Killala stands by the shore of Killala Bay where the bay water is quieted into what is veritably a still lagoon by the shelter of the long and narrow spit of Bartragh Island. 'Killala' means the church of Alaidh – 'cill' is a church – and you should pronounce it with the tonic accent on the first 'a' – kill-A'lla. The town has two vertical emphases – a round tower and the spire of the cathedral church. The round tower springs up among the houses as though it were a mill chimney in an industrial centre. It dates perhaps from the tenth century and remains from a monastery founded by St. Patrick in the fifth century. It is 84 feet high and its door is 11 feet from the ground, demonstrating in the usual manner of round towers in Ireland that uninvited visitors were not welcome.

St. Patrick appointed a bishop, Muiredach, to his monastery, and so created a see. This implied the building of a cathedral. The present Anglican church is the successor of that early cathedral and is still known by that title, though the Protestant see has long since moved to Tuam and the Catholic see to Ballina.

Killala's cathedral, despite the antiquity of the site, is not of great interest. It was built in the late seventeenth century. In the churchyard is one of those underground chambers or tunnels that in Ireland are called 'souterrains' and in Cornwall are called 'fogous', while the Scots call them 'wemys'. Their purpose seems to have been to serve as temporary refuges for people to hide in while the noise and disturbance of battle passed over their heads.

Two miles west of Killala stand the ruins of Moyne abbey, nicely situated beside the river Moy, which flows past the old, grey walls into Killala Bay. The abbey was founded by Mac William Burke in 1460 and so was not very old when the upset of the Dissolution struck it. The order for whom the abbey was built was that of the Observantine Franciscans, and the foundation was in fact properly a friary. The friars did not let the king of England worry them too much, for provincial chapters of their order were held at Moyne until 1560, and perhaps until 1590. Then Moyne was burned by Sir Richard Bingham, who had also burned Rathfran.

Moyne is a good example of the buildings of an Irish friary. It is compact, and, though it is now roofless, much remains and you may walk from room to room on two floors and in the cloister, and climb the central tower. There is an atmosphere of ghostly silence, which seems to be emphasised by the soughing of the wind. You may imagine that a file of the friars in their long robes, drawn in by a rosary or a rope at the waist, might suddenly emerge from their refectory and tread, shuffling and muttering, along the cloister garth to enter the church under the tower between the nave and the choir. In the refectory the friar who had been reading to them while they ate would put away his book and descend from his pulpit to follow them.

In the sixteenth century some idle fellow, perhaps a friar longing for a different life, took a sharp point, and scratched drawings of ships in the west wall of the nave, where they may still be seen.

If you were uncertain of the goodness of your soul or of its fate in the hereafter you might compound for your sins, and perhaps purchase a few exculpatory masses, by founding a monastery. This was perhaps the reason for the founding of yet another friary, by one William Gurnard, at the same time as Moyne just a mile or two upstream. This also was for the Observantine Franciscans. Rosserk is another good example of a sixteenth-century religious house, roofless, as Moyne is, but less complete. It has the advantage of some good carving on the west doorway, and of two angels and the Instruments of the Passion on the piscina in the chancel. But what marks Rosserk as memorable is that it has a carving of a round tower springing as from an ornamental bracket on one of the pillars of the piscina. I think that this must be unique and it would be interesting to know the reason for it, why the sculptor chose such an image at a time long before a round tower had sentimental value. And why, in particular he should have chosen to carve this image on a piscina as though it had some connection with the rites of the church.

For the visitor the name of the town of Ballina is another that requires explanation of its pronunciation. It is not, as its inhabitants must often hear, 'Ball-eena' or 'Bawl-eena'. The accent is placed on the first syllable, which is short, as 'Bally-nah'. Ballina, with two bridges over the tidal river Moy, is the best shopping-centre in Mayo, and it is also a centre for fishermen, who find salmon, sea-trout, and brown trout in the Moy and other rivers and in many lakes, including the expansive Loch Conn and its neighbour Loch Cullin, which is divided from Conn by the isthmus of Pontoon.

The Catholic cathedral at Ballina, a late nineteenth-century conventional gothic building with a spire, makes a fine accent to the river front. Next to it stand the scanty remains of an Augustinian friary founded in 1427, with a good west doorway half buried in the ground.

St. Patrick's well has been transformed into a show-piece with mosaic stations of the Cross and a figure of St. Patrick on a standing slab.

Legend describes a dolmen on the hills as the grave of the Four Maols, the Four Maols being four brothers who murdered their tutor Bishop Ceallach in the sixth century and were hanged for it on the hill of Ardnaree on the opposite side of the river. The hill bears the ruin of a fourteenth-century Augustinian church. The dolmen is of course much older than the story.

A circuit of Loch Conn is recommended, not least for its views of the bald-headed mountain of Nephin, 2446 feet high and separated from the Nephin Beg range by a small river. The mountain may be climbed for wide-spreading views of land, lake and distant sea.

There is a geological hotchpotch in this area. The summit of Nephin is whitish quartzite, like a cap of snow, the slopes are schist and gneiss and old red sandstone. Loch Conn lies for the great part in limestone, which renders the water clear and bright and of a marvellous blue under the sun. Loch Cuillin lies in granite, and the isthmus of Pontoon is of the same substance. The buildings on the isthmus include hotels and guest-houses.

Pontoon gives access to Foxford, a good fishing centre on the Moy, with a woollen industry run by the Irish Sisters of Charity. Admiral Brown, father of the Argentine navy, was born in Foxford in 1777; a bold statue of him was done by an Argentinian sculptor, Vergottini, in 1957.

Strade to Castlebar

Michael Davitt, founder of the Land League, was born at Strade, a village on the Castlebar road, in 1846. This little place has a ruined abbey or friary founded for Franciscans, but becoming Dominican in 1252. The roofless church contains sculptures that affect me deeply, a Pietà especially that haunts me with its charm and pathos. (*Plates* 27, 28.)

The piece is a triptych about four feet across. It may have been the frontal of a tomb-chest, but I think that its dimensions indicate that it was the reredos of a small altar; the absence of a frame line along the base seems to confirm this. The Virgin sits in the centre, under two canted ogee arches, with the limp body of Christ on her lap. She is guarded by two feathered flying angels. The two flanking niches contain figures that I like to think are St. Joseph (or St. John) and Mary Magdalene.

This piece has remarkable qualities that distinguish it from other works of the middle ages in Ireland. An elaborate tomb-chest in this same ruined church at Strade has similarities of style and workmanship, but I believe it to be rather of the same school than by the same hand. The Pietà has a refreshing naturalism with a deep sense of humanity; it avoids pretentiousness and display. Mary is not the crowned queen of Heaven, nor the great lady that many artists of the middle ages and the Renaissance loved to show, as for example Jan van Eyck's richly gowned Virgin appearing to the hard-faced Chancellor Rollin, nor Jean Fouquet's clinically posed portrait of Agnes Sorel as the Virgin. The Virgin at Strade is more akin to Gerard David's peasant woman feeding her child with a wooden spoon. David and the sculptor of Strade remembered that Mary was the wife of a carpenter and a poor woman of simple circumstances; the Strade sculptor has clearly gone to the local people for both the features and the costume of his characters. He shows Mary with a plain wimple on her head, worn as the shawl is still worn in Ireland, and he dresses her in a collarless gown that lacks all ornament other than the fluted folds in which the double skirt hangs. She is any one of many women whose sons have been killed by violence or at sea – she is Maurya of Synge's *Riders to the Sea*, for example. She looks down grieving at the body on her knees, which she supports with one hand under the head and the other holding a wrist, avoiding a nail hole. The body is limp, as you may see by the bend of the elbow, the lax folding of the knees, and the droop of the pierced feet.

As though to emphasise the weight of her sorrow the sculptor has set a burden upon Mary by making her into a caryatid, with a wedge-shaped block on her head that is the respond for the two canted ogee arches and at the same time the base of a sturdy pinnacle. The arches are filled by the flying angels, who are feathered not only on the wings but all over their bodies – a not uncommon medieval conceit.

The two side niches are contained under triangular heads as heavily crocketed and pinnacled as are the ogees. The kneeling figure on the left, with arms raised and palms forward, in the posture of an orante, I suppose to be either Joseph of Arimathea or John the beloved disciple. His curly hair is characteristic of many Irishmen of the west to this day, and it strengthens the supposition that the sculptor went to local people for his models. The figure wears a garment that resembles a medieval *cote-hardie*, with a frontal descending before the belt to end in a sharp horizontal above a stiffened and pleated skirt or kilt. The buttons seen on the left of the skirt may represent a rosary hanging from the belt. Also hanging from the belt is a cigar-shaped object with lateral lines; it has been suggested to me that this is a scrip or purse such as pilgrims carried, in which case the lines might represent the lacing of the opening, but it would have been a very inconveniently shaped receptacle. Similar buttons and another 'scrip' are seen on a figure on the neighbouring tomb-chest.

The sculptor seems to have taken pains and especial delight in expressing both the physical charm and the holiness of the figure in the right-hand niche of the Pietà, and for this reason I suppose her to be the Magdalene. She is a remarkable figure, in sharp contrast with the sadness of the Virgin. All her lines are sensuous curves, from the fall of her long hair to the folds of her gown or cloak, but the effect is not that of a wanton.

Her face has the pleased Mona Lisa expression of a woman nursing a secret, as though in the presence of the dead Christ she is sure already of the coming resurrection. She is shown half kneeling and this movement has given the sculptor the opportunity to study the thick folds of her heavy garment. Her hands appear at first sight to be crossed on her breast, but in fact they are folded in prayer and are turned sideways simply to avoid the projection of the stone that would otherwise have been necessary. The many-buttoned sleeves are characteristic of many medieval garments that have been found preserved in the peat bogs of Ireland and are now in the National Museum in Dublin.

The date of this Pietà is not as obvious as it may appear. The ogee arches and the pinnacles clearly suggest the fourteenth century, as also do the buttoned sleeves, but fashion in Ireland, especially in architecture, lagged a long way behind England. What is seen in Ireland as the full flower of the Decorated period may be contemporary with England's Perpendicular. The fourteenth century, in any case, is too early, for it would place the Pietà among the earliest works of the sort and this is not credible. I believe that the Strade Pietà should be attributed to the latter part of the fifteenth century.

At Castlebar, General Humbert, with his French and Irish forces, inflicted that sharp reverse on the British under General Lake. John Moore, the rebel president of Connacht, and General Humbert had their headquarters in the Humbert Inn. Moore is buried in the tree-lined Mall near the monument to the rebels of 1798.

Castlebar is the administrative capital of the county of Mayo. There is indeed a place called Mayo, from which the county has its name, but though once the site of an important monastery, it is now a mere hamlet on a minor road south of Balla. Castlebar is a pleasant town of colour-washed houses, and a good fishing centre. It is surrounded by lochs, many of them small, but productive, and others large, from Loch Conn in the north to Lochs Mask and Corrib in the south.

For at least twelve years, about the end of each June, Castlebar has held an international four-day walk. Walkers from all over Europe and even from the U.S.A. gather in the town with packs on their backs and heavy boots on their feet, hail old acquaintances and start off on their long-distance trek. No-one need do more than he wants, for the route is divided into sections to suit all ages and all abilities. There is beautiful scenery to be enjoyed and good Irish food, and the fellowship of the open road.

From Castlebar we may make our way back to Westport by the T39, or continue south by the T40 by Ballinrobe and Headford to Galway.

A mile east of the T40 stands the abbey of Ballintubber, the 'town of the well', where St. Patrick baptised his converts in a holy well and founded a church. The abbey was founded on the site of the church in 1216 for Canons Regular of the order of St. Augustine, by Cathal Crovdearg, King of Connacht – Cathal of the Wine-red Hand. The abbey was nominally suppressed in 1542, and was attacked and burnt by Cromwellian soldiery in 1653; but the chancel of the church retained its stone vault and services of the Mass continued. Now the church, restored between 1963 and 1966, can claim that mass has been said here without a break for at least 750 years, and for much longer if one counts Patrick's fifth-century church. The building is stern, with little ornament, but imposing, with bright modern glass in the windows, and it is well worth a visit. (*Plate* 26.)

There was a pilgrim path, the Tóchar Phádraig, from Ballintubber to the holy mountain of Croagh Patrick, which may still be traced, with the cone of the mountain visible in the distance as a guide.

Just to the south of the abbey lies Loch Carra, on the east shore of which the novelist George Moore, born in 1852, lived in Moore Hall. Moore was buried on an island in the lake. Moore Hall is now a ruin, burned in 1923, and the demesne is given over to forestry.

The fretted shores of Loch Carra are divided by the isthmus of Partry from the more open water of Loch Mask. The eastern shore of the loch is limestone, the west the harder and earlier strata of the Partry Mountains, which rise on Maumtrasna to 2207 feet. Ballinrobe is the fishing and touring centre for this district, and fishermen may rejoice that in Lochs Corrib and Mask (as also in Lochs Conn and Cullin) they have free waters for their sport. The town is a local shopping centre. The parish church contains nine good windows by the Harry Clarke Studio. There are scanty remains of an Augustinian friary and a medieval church. Race meetings occur in April and June, and a drama festival and an agricultural show. Scattered about the district are various antiquities, including stone forts and cairns, and castles, and the structure called 'the Gods of the Neale'. Neale, pronounced 'Nail', is a pleasant little village south of Ballinrobe, beside the demesne of Neale House. In the grounds of the house are 'the Gods', a structure of medieval tomb carvings, with a queer nineteenth-century inscription, taking 'the Gods' back to 'the year of the world 2994'. Other curiosities in the demesne include a stepped pyramid known as the Weathercock.

The district about here is the Plain of Moytura, claimed to be the site of one of the two battles in which the De Danaan defeated the Fir Bolg. Sir William Wilde, the father of Oscar Wilde, studied this area in detail and gave fanciful names to its features and remains which you may read about in his book.

Loughmask House, to the west of the Neale, near the lake (the house is still inhabited) was the home of Captain Boycott, agent for Lord Erne. Boycott so irritated Lord Erne's tenants that, under the inspiration of Parnell, they revolted against him. They would not deliver his post, nor supply him with goods, nor work in his house nor on his estate; and so a new word, 'to boycott', came into the English language.

The road through Headford to Galway is now straightforward.

9
County Sligo

Whether the county of Sligo is part of the west or of the north-west depends, of course, on your point of view. For the Sligo man can look west not only to the Atlantic, but to another county that is farther west than his own. He can look into Mayo, and he can look south-west into Connemara in county Galway. There are those who would affirm that nothing east of the Galway-Mayo border is really the 'west' and some who seem to believe that only Connemara and perhaps Murrisk is the true west of Ireland, the place that is meant when the west is in question. It depends. It depends what you want to do and what you want to explore, what you want to believe. For me the 'west' includes the splendid county of Sligo, which, although it lies against the borders of Donegal, the most northerly county in Ireland, and close by the marches of Ulster, is included in the western province of Connacht.

I like county Sligo, I like its open beaches, I like the great jutting tablelands of its hills and mountains, I like its lakes and glens, and I like its people, and the contrast between the solitary hills and the strands, and the metropolitan busyness of the little town of Sligo itself.

You might say that the county begins and ends with seaside resorts. There is Enniscrone on Killala Bay at one end and Bundoran at the other, which is not in county Sligo at all but just over the border, or in fact two borders, but is near enough to count. Between the genteel Enniscrone, trying to be more popular, and Bundoran, which is too popular for the taste of some people, lies a totally different kind of country.

In the last chapter we turned southwards in Ballina for Castlebar and Claremorris, on our way to Galway. To include county Sligo in our itinerary we go east in Ballina across the river Moy, to follow the river shore from the point where the water begins to widen and to become an estuary inhabited by salmon and sea-trout, which come exploring upstream from the shallow waters of Killala Bay.

Enniscrone to Ballysodare.

Enniscrone, or Inishcrone, is a seaside resort with a long, long sandy strand extending along the eastern shore of the bay. The sea-bathing is good, and in addition there are establishments with remedial sulphur baths and so forth. The usual seaside architecture predominates, with obvious holiday hotels and flats close by the smaller kind of house typical of Irish towns anywhere, vaguely Georgian in style. The outdoors is represented by a marina, a pier for fishing-boats, and a golf-course by the sea, and indoor gaiety by a ballroom. (*Plate* 25.)

Two miles north, as shown on the map but it is not in fact obvious on the ground, stood Lecan castle, or the castle of Firbis, which was the home of the Firbis family, notable as poets and annalists. About 1390 they compiled the Yellow Book of Lecan, which is now in the library of Trinity College, Dublin, and they also wrote The Great Book of Lecan, which is in the Royal Irish Academy, also in Dublin. Descended from Daithi, the last pagan king of Ireland, the Mac Firbis were a scholarly line. They ended when the last of the family was stabbed to death in an inn farther along this coast.

At Easky, still following the sea, but at a distance, the road has turned east and will now follow that general direction for many miles. A tall and solid tower-house, Roslee, stands by the sea with its feet in the water. It is reached by a bohreen. Mac Donnells lived here, in this tower-house, looking out over Donegal Bay to the headland of Malinbegs and Killybegs. The beach next to the tower is a litter of rocks and pebbles, and you need not look far to find many different sizes of a strange kind of pebble, a curiosity for the geologist. A typical example is of hard grey limestone pierced with hundreds of closely gathered white rods about an eighth of an inch to a quarter of an inch in diameter. The Department of the Geological Survey of Ireland tells me that these grey and white pebbles, so strikingly patterned, are of limestone containing corals, and that they were formed in warm water at shallow depths about 350 million years ago. (*Plate* 19.)

Two Martello towers are evidence of an unlikely belief that Napoleon might choose to invade on this lonely coast – but the possibility would have seemed more likely to those who remembered the invasion of General Humbert at Lacken Bay not so very many years previously.

East of Easky, by the roadside, lies the Split Rock, or 'Fionn Mac Cumhail's Finger-Stone'. 'Finger-Stone' seems an inappropriate title, for the rock is a huge, round, isolated boulder, as big as a house, divided by a vertical split as straight as a knife. The legends conflict. One says that Fionn split the rock with his sword. Another says that Fionn tried to hurl the stone into the sea, but did not throw hard enough. In a rage he threw a second stone, which struck the first and split it.

Between Easky and Ballysodare, south of Sligo, there is nothing but small villages, and about them many early antiquities, nearly all in a ruined state. Inland rise the Slieve Gamph, otherwise called the Ox Mountains, of hard intrusive granite, gneiss, schist, and quartzite, with Knockalongy reaching 1778 feet. Up among them, accessible by road from Dromore West, is Loch Easky, a place for fishermen to exult in remoteness, and perhaps to catch a fish into the bargain. Dromore West is a tree-embowered village where the Dunneil river comes out of the mountains to tumble over a modest but pretty waterfall, and pass beneath the Sligo road. The ruined church in the village became Protestant in 1616 and was abandoned in 1818.

On the coast, Aughris Head has a large sandy strand sloping up to sand dunes, a place to have the sea and the world to yourself. It looks out over the sea to Raghly Point and to Rosses Point beside Drumcliff Bay. Inland the dramatic cliffs of Knocknarea front the sea above Strandhill, and beyond is Ben Bulben, with its flat and vertical cliff and shawl of scree.

Skreen is where the last of the Firbis was stabbed to death by a country fellow in a tavern. He found the presence of the old scribe a hindrance to his courtship of a serving-wench.

Above Skreen a minor road climbs into the mountains over Ladies' Brae, passing Loch Achree. The lake, hidden from the road by rising ground, is called Ireland's youngest lake, for the barrage holding back the water was formed in 1490 by an earthquake.

At Dromard it is worth while to make a detour south to find Longford House. The house, of Georgian origin, is of no great interest, but let in the demesne wall and approached by a stile, is a strange little building, a kind of garden folly or perhaps a chapel, whose walls are lined with sculptured figures which stare at you with pop eyes. The figures represent the Crucifixion, the Virgin and Child, and various saints. They may belong to the seventeenth century.

As you pass Beltra and come to Ballysodare, following around Ballysodare Bay, Knocknarea shows beyond the water, changing shape as you move, from a cliff-girt mountain – which, surprisingly, is only

1078 feet high but looks much more – into a rounded summit like a breast, topped with a prominent nipple. The nipple is the great cairn of Misgaun Méabh. We shall say more of it shortly.

We have arrived in Ballysodare in the Yeats country, or in the northern Yeats country, the countryside where William Butler Yeats spent much of his formative years, absorbing traditions and folklore that were to be transferred to his verse. The Pollexfen family, his mother's family, frequently received him at their house.

In Ballysodare Yeats heard an old woman singing and out of that came the poem 'Down by the sally gardens'. In Ireland 'sally' is a common word for the willow tree – it is the English 'sallow'.

The first impression of Ballysodare is of industry from the great flour mill, with its corrugated iron and concrete rising beside the river; but the river is clear and contains salmon. It flows over ledges of rock in a series of shallow falls that have given the town its name – 'Baile Easa Daire' means the town of the waterfall of the oak tree. On the western bank, near the mouth of the river, are the remains of a monastery founded in the seventh century by St. Fechin of Fore. It includes Teampall Feichna, with a romanesque doorway in an earlier building, and a thirteenth-century church built after the community became Augustinian.

Sligo to Knocknarea

Sligo is a more lively and busier town than the number of its population of about fifteen hundred persons might suggest. It is the only such place in the county and is, of course, the county capital. it has Catholic and Anglican cathedrals. It grew here on this particular site because the river Garavogue, coming out of Loch Gill, was fordable over slabs of rock at this point. A castle built in 1245 to guard the ford was destroyed and rebuilt more than once. In 1414 the town and the priory were destroyed by fire. In the Cromwellian wars Sligo was twice taken by the English. In the Williamite war it was for a time in the hands of Patrick Sarsfield.

The bridge at the centre of the town marks the site of the ford. Beneath it swans struggle against the current and along the slabby course of the river keen anglers, ranging from young boys to mature men, stand posed with their rods, hoping for a salmon or a trout – in places fishing in the river is free. The parapets of the bridge give convenient support for the elbows of the many spectators. (*Plate* 16.)

Sligo, except for its ruined priory, is not architecturally distinguished.

The City Hall, built in 1864, is a neo-Byzantine-romanesque building; at the foot of Quay Street, in which it stands, a net is drawn across the river at certain times of the day in the hope of trapping salmon. The most interesting modern building is the massively constructed railway station, an essay in purposeful design.

The Anglican cathedral of St. Mary the Virgin and St. John the Baptist was built in 1739 to the design of Richard Cassels, the German architect we have previously met and who did much work in Ireland, notably in Dublin. A good building as he left it, it was not improved by gothicisation by a later hand in 1812. It contains a brass memorial to Susan Mary Yeats, mother of the poet W.B. Yeats and of the artist Jack B. Yeats - who for long was overshadowed by the fame of his brother, but is now recognised. The adjacent churchyards of the Anglican cathedral and of the Catholic cathedral of the Immaculate Conception are divided only by a stone wall.

The former Dominican priory, known as Sligo abbey, founded in 1252, was burned out in the fire of 1414, and was afterwards rebuilt. Some thirteenth-century details remain, but the building, or what remains of it, is mostly of the fifteenth century. The priory was destroyed by Cromwellians in 1641 and has been a ruin since. The roofless church, three sides of the cloister, and some domestic buildings remain. In the nave is a graceful monument of 1506 to Cormac O Craian and his wife Aecca, and opposite it is an interesting renaissance monument for Sir Donchadh O Connor, who died in 1624; this latter monument was put up by his wife, who is shown kneeling by her husband.

West of the town the Garavogue river flows into a broad bay floored with the wide and level sands of Cumeen Strand, an expanse mentioned by Yeats in Red Hanrahan's Song - 'The old brown thorn tree breaks in two High over Cumeen Strand'. The bay is almost closed at its mouth by the low-lying Coney Island - only half an island, for the channel to the south is dry at low tide and you may walk over, guided by posts.

At the point of the peninsula south of Coney Island, St. Patrick consecrated one of his disciples, Bronius, as bishop. The ruined church of Killaspugbrón is an early building within a square churchyard wall - Killaspugbrón means the church of Bishop Bron. While he was here St. Patrick lost a tooth. The account does not say what miseries the saint suffered from a broken or rotten tooth, but surely, at that time and in that remote place, toothache must have been an agony not easily allayed. The fallen tooth was seized upon as a relic to be revered, and later a shrine was made for it, the Fiacail Phádraig, the tooth of Patrick. In the fourteenth century this shrine was elaborately enriched. It may be seen today, without the tooth for which it was made, in the National Museum in Dublin.

As for the church, it retains a treasure in the splendid views it affords of Knocknarea to the south and of Ben Bulben northwards. Caravanners by the shore not far away and golfers on Strandhill's famous golf-course enjoy equivalent views.

Strandhill is a small village that has become known locally as a seaside resort. It has a long sandy strand on which the sea flings cohorts of rollers that are the delight of surfers. An old house, Dolly's Cottage, has been restored and as a typical nineteenth-century rural dwelling is open to the public in the summer, with a programme of Irish entertainment on certain evenings.

Above the village rise the sheer, grey cliffs of Knocknarea, which seem to deny access to the hills; but a leafy glen penetrates among them, and the top may be reached by unexpectedly easy slopes behind the cliff. On top is a huge cairn of stone that is visible over a distance of many miles as the nipple on the round breast of Knocknarea.

'Knocknarea' means the hill of the kings, but the cairn bears the name of a queen, Méabh or Maeve, who was a queen in Sligo somewhere about the beginning of our era. She appears in legend as the queen who initiated the great cattle raid of Cooley, an attempt to invade northwards and steal a famous bull that belonged to the king of Ulster. Alone the hero Cuchullain defended Ulster. The story, the Táin Bo Cuailgne, appears in two ancient manuscripts, *The Book of the Dun Cow* and *The Book of Leinster*, both in Trinity College, Dublin. In 1975, Thomas Kinsella, the poet, published a translation of the epic. Known simply as The Táin, the story is one of the great tales of Irish legend.

Misgain Méabh, the cairn on Knocknarea, in fact long outdates the queen whose name is attached to it; it probably belongs to the bronze age and covers a passage grave. No-one has opened it to find out, and when you look at this great cairn, the size of a pyramid, you will understand why; a great deal of money and a great deal of labour, with the destruction of the structure, would be involved. The difficulties have preserved the cairn intact through four thousand years. The same thing is true of the similar cairn at Heapstown by the north shore of Loch Arrow.

In the meadowlands east of Knocknarea is the megalithic cemetery of

Carrowmore, an extraordinary place where antiquities of the bronze age lie thick on the ground. For some reason we no longer know, perhaps because Knocknarea was deemed a holy place, the nobles of the time chose to have their sepulture here in these fields. Dolmens or cromlechs, stone circles – some of them the kerbs of former cairns or vanished tumuli – and standing stones, are scattered everywhere in this ground. There used to be about two hundred of them; about sixty remain, the bare stones of an ancient culture. Even on a sunny spring day one feels something weird in the atmosphere of Carrowmore. (*Plate* 24.)

W. B. Yeats and Loch Gill

East of Sligo lies Loch Gill, the jewel of the county, which is frequently compared with Killarney for the beauty of its islands and wooded shores. The river Bonet flows in at its eastern end from the region of Manorhamilton and the wild valley of Glenade, and the Garavogue flows out to the west through the middle of the town of Sligo. A circuit of the lake by road is a favourite and worthwhile excursion. Alternatively, you may hire a boat in Sligo and sail the five-mile length of the lake, passing Church Island, where Saint Loman founded a monastery in the sixth century, ruins of which still stand. A hollowed rock is called Our Lady's Bed and is said to confer easy childbirth upon women who lie on it. But the most famous of the islands in the lake is the most insignificant, so small that it does not appear on the half-inch map. 'Inisfree' means the island of heather, and it is famous because Yeats made it so by choosing it as the subject of one of his best-loved poems, the brief and nostalgic 'I will arise and go now, and go to Inisfree'.

At the south-western corner of the lake a country park has been made around the foot of Dooney Rock, the rocky promontory rising from the shore, which Yeats mentions in his poem, 'The Fiddler of Dooney'. There is a car-park now beside the road, and a picnic site with the usual rustic tables and benches. Various paths go down to the lake shore and around the base of the rock, and others climb steeply among the trees to look-out platforms on the summit, with good views of Church Island and of Cottage Island and beyond the lake to the knobbly uplands of Crockauns and the limestone cliffs of King's Mountain and of Ben Bulben – Yeats lies buried beneath the latter at Drumcliff.

Between Dooney Rock and the hill of Slish Wood a stream flows into the lake through a gap made by a glacier and the road follows this away from the shore. This wood is the 'Sleuth Wood' of Yeats's 'The Stolen

Child'. The road goes on to cross the Bonet at Dromahair, where Yeats placed the man who dreamed of fairyland. Dromahair is a small town, once the capital of the O Rourke princes of Breifne. In O Rourke's castle here Devorgilla, O Rourke's wife, began an affair with Dermot Mac Murrough, King of Leinster – or perhaps she was kidnapped by Mac Murrough. Whether Devorgilla was innocent or no, the incident sparked off a chain of events that led to the Normans being invited into Ireland by Mac Murrough, and started the centuries-long conflict between the English and the Irish the effects of which are still evident in Northern Ireland. The hill called O Rourke's Table, north of the town, is where, in a sentimental poem, Tom Moore imagined O Rourke mourning over the loss of his wife.

Part of O Rourke's castle remains at Dromahair, conjoined with the remains of a seventeenth-century plantation castle of the Villiers family. Not far away stands Creevelea friary founded in 1508 by Margaret, wife of Eoghan O Rourke, for Franciscans. As was frequently the case with Irish monastic houses, the Dissolution was not final here and the friars were still occupying the friary in 1642 and later. The buildings, one of the latest examples of a pre-Reformation monastery, are largely complete, though roofless.

St. Patrick is said to have founded the church at the nearby Drumlease, but the present ruins are unlikely to be of his time.

The road follows the eastern and northern shore of the lake and passes Parke's castle between road and water. It is a fortified house rather than a true castle and was built by a seventeenth-century planter, a man from England who hoped to settle and live on an estate here in the west of Ireland. As you may see by the fortifications of the castle, he could not have anticipated a life of peace, though from his windows he might have enjoyed beautiful views of the calm lake on whose shores he had set his closely walled house with its strong defences of drum towers.

North of the lake at Magheranrush, or the Deerpark, is court cairn, standing on a hill with a view over the water, and indeed all around, as far as the Dartry Mountains, which include Ben Bulben but rise to their highest point at 2120 feet on the summit of Truskmore. A court cairn is one with a courtyard of stones at one end, built for some ceremony or purpose that we do not know. Much of this one has disappeared, but the entrances were lintelled until the nineteenth century and this caused it to be known as the Irish Stonehenge. The cairn is probably of neolithic date.

A peninsula at the western end of the lake comprises the demesne of Hazelwood, with an eighteenth-century house designed by Richard Cassels. The house has had various uses.

North of Sligo town, in a rift between the mountains and the hills, lies the pretty valley of Glencar, a place familiar to Yeats, who wrote 'The Stolen Child' about it and mentioned the waterfall with its pools that 'scarce could bathe a star'. The road along the north side of the valley passes Glencar Lake and also the waterfall, which is reached by bridges and a concrete path crossing over the tumbling little stream, and sidling by rhododendrons, whose colourful flowers confer an exotic beauty to the view of the fall.

The grey limestone cliffs seen from the region of the glen belong to King's Mountain, which you may easily mistake for Ben Bulben, the next prow to the north.

Another waterfall coming down from the mountain side is called Sruh-in-aghaidh-an-Áird, which means the stream against the height; in certain conditions a strong wind will lift the water back against the slope and give the impression of a waterfall flowing upwards.

The road through this attractive valley leads to Manorhamilton, a small town where in 1638 Sir Frederick Hamilton built a large and strongly fortified house; the house still stands, but as a ruin covered with ivy. But in coming through Glencar we have crossed the county border into Leitrim. To stay in county Sligo we must turn back down the glen from the waterfall to the main road again at Drumcliff.

St. Columcille founded a monastery at Drumcliff in the sixth century in repentance for an unsaintly deed that ended in the deaths of many men. Columcille, while a guest with St. Finian, borrowed his host's manuscript of the Bible and secretly copied part of it. Finian found out and demanded the copy as his property. Columcille refused to hand it over. The matter was referred to the high king, who found for Finian; but so attached was Columcille to his copy, or to the principle of the right to copy, he gathered an army and met the king's forces in battle at Cooldrumman below Ben Bulben. He won the day. Tardily, he regretted what he had done and took himself off to Iona to live a more saintly life and to found the abbey of Iona.

Ben Bulben and Drumcliff

The book written out by Columcille, called the Cathach, was for centuries the talisman of the O Donnells, carried to their many battles to ensure victory; it has survived fourteen hundred eventful years and is now in the library of the Royal Irish Academy in Dublin.

Of Columcille's monastery at Drumcliff nothing remains but the lower part of a round tower later than his time, and, set in the churchyard wall, a fine carved high cross. W. B. Yeats's great grandfather, John Yeats, was rector of the plain Georgian gothic church from 1805. His father, John B. Yeats, married Susan Pollexfen of Sligo, whose memorial we have noticed in the cathedral of St. John in Sligo town. The poet spent much of his childhood at the Pollexfen's house. These associations made him wish to be buried at Drumcliff. He died at Roquebrune in the south of France in 1939 and his body brought to Drumcliff in 1948. He lies under a simple headstone, inexpertly lettered:

> *Cast a cold eye*
> *On Life, on Death,*
> *Horseman, pass by.*

The road west from Drumcliff passes Lissadell, the italianate mansion of the Gore-Booth family. The house, in a large, wooded demesne, is open to the public. The family derives from Sir Francis Gore, an Elizabethan soldier, who had a castle at the nearby Ardtermon, the ruins of which still stand. The present house, near the shore of Drumcliff Bay, was built in 1830-36. Yeats was a frequent visitor here and described the two daughters of the house, Constance and Eva, as 'two girls in silk kimonos, Both beautiful, one a gazelle'. Eva wrote poetry, some of which finds its way into anthologies. Constance married and became the Countess Markievicz; deeply interested in the cause of Irish freedom, she won a parliamentary seat for Sinn Fein, the first woman to be elected to the British Parliament. She chose to sit, however, in the revolutionary parliament, the Dáil, in Dublin, and did not take her seat at Westminster.

When you visit Lissadell, it is likely to be one of the Gore-Booth family who will show you round the splendid rooms, which look out on to the sea, on to Knocknarea, and on to Ben Bulben.

There are lonely yellow strands about Raghly and along the shore beyond, strands that were littered with corpses when ships of the Spanish Armada, desperately seeking their way home to Spain round Ireland, went down in storms off this coast.

Four miles off the coast, reached by hiring a boat from Grange or from Rosses Point, lies Inishmurray, an island inhabited until a few years ago.

It is stuffed full with antiquities relating to a Celtic monastery founded at some uncertain date, but apparently coming to an end with a Viking raid in the year 807. The monastery has a pear-shaped enclosing wall or cashel, which contains a number of buildings, including early churches and clocháns, together with lettered stones asking for prayers, cross slabs, stations, and memorials (called *leachtaí* and *tratháin*), and a set of inscribed stones known as *clocha breacha*, the speckled stones. By turning these stones with the appropriate maledictions unpleasant things might be made to happen to one's enemies. During the centuries they lived on the island the islanders made use of the old monastic buildings – an ancient oratory as a chapel, for instance. Teampall Mo Laisse, the church of the founder of the monastery, became a chapel especially for the men, and Teampall Mhuire, Mary's church, a chapel for the women. Inishmurray seems to retain a palpable ambience of the people, now departed, who inhabited the island for so long,

Beyond Grange, the road, the T18, runs northward, inland from the coast, to Cliffoney and Creevykeel. At Creevy-keel there is a famous example of a neolithic court cairn, much reduced in height but showing the plan clearly. In the centre it has a large open court, beyond which is a double burial chamber. Yet another burial chamber, entered from the side, may be a later addition. The cairn was excavated in 1935, when polished stone axes, flint tools, etc., were discovered.

A road turning north-east near the cairn runs up into the heart of the Dartry Mountains and round a great, natural amphitheatre below Truskmore. This is Gleniff. There is a cave up there, not very accessible, reputed one of the sleeping-places of Diarmuid and Gráinne as they fled throughout Ireland before the wrath of King Fionn Mac Cumhail. This story of an Irish Tristram and Iseult began when the king entrusted Diarmuid with a mission to collect Gráinne, Fionn's bride. Instead of conveying her safely home Diarmuid stole her away. If you will believe the legend the pair slept in the most unlikely places and never could a wooing have been less comfortable. Caves and hollows and dozens of dolmens or cromlechs throughout Ireland are called 'Diarmuid and Gráinne's bed' – there is, for example the Labby, a dolmen in the Moytura district near Loch Arrow, with an extraordinarily ponderous capstone weighing about forty tons – preparing such a bed would have been nothing for an Irish hero! The name, the 'Labby', comes from the Irish word for 'bed' – 'leabaidh'.

Diarmuid was eventually killed by trickery by Fionn while feigning friendship, and Grainne then made no bones about becoming his queen. She was perhaps longing for a good night's sleep in a soft bed.

North of Cliffony a rocky peninsula juts out into Donegal Bay. Mullaghmore on this peninsula is a small resort with a good bay and a sandy strand, and a road running above cliffs. A house standing prominently on a headland and dominating the landscape and the sea is Classiebawn castle, a Victorian gothic mansion built in 1874 and in 1979 a residence of Earl Mountbatten of Burma. In that year he and members of his family were killed by a bomb attack by the I.R.A. on his boat in the bay.

A few miles farther on, Sligo comes to an end where county Leitrim extends a narrow strip of a couple of miles to the sea, scarcely enough to give Leitrim a claim to be considered a maritime county. Then comes another county border, with Donegal, and a coastwise strip along which runs the T18 road through Bundoran to link Donegal with the rest of the republic. To the east is the boundary of Northern Ireland.

We make our way back to Sligo town, passing the turn to Rosses Point, where there is a fine strand of sand and a famous eighteen-hole championship golf course opposite the channel dividing Coney Island from the mainland. A week-end sea festival takes place here in the summer, with sea-angling and boating events. On Black Rock the Metal Man warns boats of the danger of rocks.

Sligo also has its festival, in July, when there are show-jumping, agricultural events, craftsmanship and cooking competitions, exhibitions, and so on. For four weeks in July the Yeats English Language School teaches English and a knowledge of Anglo-Irish literature to foreign students. A different event in August is the Yeats International Summer School, when lectures and discussions centre round the work of W. B. Yeats. The Sligo museum is a museum of general Sligo interest, but it also has an interesting section of Yeatsiana, including manuscripts, early editions, photographs, and the medal of the Nobel prize for literature awarded to Yeats in 1923.

South of Sligo town beyond Ballysodare the road divides at Collooney. The Ballysodare river comes through the Collooney gap, and indeed helped geologically to form it, and the road and the railway follow this line. The gap was an obvious route for armies and invaders and there was a castle to defend the way. Among the battles fought for the gap was that of 1798, in which General Humbert's French forces defeated the British, on their way to the triumph of 'the races of Castlebar'; a monument on a hill commemorates the bravery of a Captain Teeling in the battle. Markree, south-east of the village, is a Georgian mansion altered in Gothic fashion in 1803 by Francis Johnston; its owner was an enthusiastic astronomer and once possessed the largest telescope in the British Isles. The telescope has gone elsewhere but the building that housed it is still here.

The T3 south-east goes up past the modest Bricklieve Mountains, where a group of strange antiquities – megaliths and stone huts – at Carrowkeel stand high on a ridge that gives panoramic views of Loch Arrow. A few miles east is an isolated hill called Keshcorran, with a series of caves in which were discovered various prehistoric remains and bones of animals long extinct in Ireland. In one of these caves, tradition says, echoing Roman legend, an Irish hero, Cormac Mac Airt, was suckled by a she-wolf.

From Kesh we go westwards by minor roads, through Ballymote, where there was a castle long disputed between the English and the Irish, until the followers of William II captured it and dismantled it. It was a keepless castle, not a tower-house, with strong circular towers. Its ruins remain, covered with ivy. Nearby are the remains of a Franciscan friary, whose inhabitants in the fourteenth century compiled *The Book of Ballymote*, five hundred pages of legend and history, now in the library of the Irish Academy in Dublin.

The road west leads to the T11 and this goes south through Tobercurry into Mayo to Ballyhaunis. A few miles west from here will take you to Knock, one of the most extraordinary places in Ireland. Extraordinary, yet physically a very ordinary, commonplace country village. But here on the 21 of August 1879 something remarkable occurred. The Virgin Mary, no less, appeared in broad daylight against the gable of the church, together with St. Joseph and St. John, and a lamb with a cross, the familiar Agnus Dei. Two women saw them first and thought the priest must have brought in some statues, but when the women passed again later they saw that the 'statues' were moving. The women called other people to see the figures, which, no transient vision, remained in view for a considerable time. They called the priest too, through his housekeeper – but the priest was busy, and thinking some delusion must be in question, a trick of the light, perhaps, he did not come. What is sure is that many inhabitants of Knock came and saw the figures and had time to discuss them. Explain that away if you can. I cannot.

Knock is now a place of pilgrimage and scores of thousands of devout men and women come to kneel in the hard yard and to pray at the shrine that has been built where the figures were seen. Facilities for the pilgrims have had to be provided on a grand scale. Holy water comes from chromium-plated taps like mains taps. There are public lavatories – among the most extensive and the cleanest in Ireland, and parks for cars and coaches. Knock is one of the great pilgrim centres, to which the devout aspire from all over Ireland. Many people come repeatedly.

We are in the district called the Plains of Mayo. Southwards the road goes to Claremorris, a railway junction and a market town, with its main street gently climbing to its two churches, Anglican and Catholic, neither of particular interest, though the Catholic church has some pleasant revival glass. Shortly afterwards we come to the county boundary on the way to Tuam and the main road to the city of Galway.

The Meaning of Irish Place-Names

Many Irish place names owe their origin to common Gaelic usage and are easily understandable to the Gaelic reader. But they have been complicated by attempts to render them with English spellings. In modern Ireland both the anglicised spelling and the Gaelic spelling appear on signposts. In the following examples the anglicised spelling of prefixes and other elements appears first, with the Gaelic spelling following in italics, and then the meaning in English.

agh, agh, augh, *achadh*, a field
aglish, *eaglais*, a church
ah, atha, *áth*, a ford
all, ail, *aill*, a cliff
anna, eanna, *éanach*, a marsh
ard, ar, *árd*, a height
as, ess, *eas*, a waterfall
aw, ow, *abha*, a river; *see also* owen
bal, bel, *béal*, the mouth (of a river or valley)
bal, balli, bally, *baile*, a town
ballagh, balla, *bealach*, a way or path
bawn, bane, *bán*, white
barn, *bearna*, a gap
beg, *beag*, small
boola, booley, *buaile*, booleying, i. e. the movement of cattle from
   lowland to hill pastures; summer pasture
boy, *buidhe*, yellow
bun, *bun*, the foot or bottom (of a valley) or the mouth of a river
caher, cahir, *cathair*, a fort, a city
carrick, carrig, corrig, *carraig*, a rock
cashel, *caiseal*, a castle

clogh, *cloich*, a stone

clon, clun, *cluain*, a meadow

derg, *dearg*, red

doo, du, duv, duf, *dubh*, black

dun, *dún*, a fort

glan, glen, *gleann*, a valley

illaun, *oileán*, an island

inch, inish, *inis*, an island; or *inse*, a river meadow

knock, *cnoc*, a hill; the *k* should properly be pronounced, and in the west
   usual!y is; elsewhere it may be silent as in English 'knock, know'

ken, kin, can, *ceann*, a headland or the head of something

kil, kill, *cill*, a church; usually at the beginning of a name, e.g. Killarney;
   or *caol*, narrow, usually at the end, e.g. Kilkeel. Sometimes *coill*, a
   wood.

lis, liss, *lios*, a fort

lough, *loch*, a lake or sea inlet

ma, may, moy, *magh*, a plain

mone, mona, *móna*, turf or a turf bog

monaster, *mainistir*, a monastery

more, mor, *mór*, big or great

owen, avon, *abhainn*, a river

rath, *rath*, a ring-fort

rinn, reen, *rinn*, a point

roe, *ruadh*, red

ross, ros, *ros*, a peninsula, a wood

see, *suidhe*, a seat; in several mountains called Seefin, Fin's seat

shan, shane, *sean*, old

slieve, *sliabh*, a mountain, or *sléibhte*, mountains

tir, tyr, *tír*, country

tubber, tobrid, tubbrid, *tobar*, a well

tra, traw, *tráigh* or *trá*, a strand or beach

Bibliography

Books for reference and further reading

Guide to the National Monuments of Ireland by Peter Harbison. Gill and Macmillan, Dublin. Stone and earthwork structures arranged by counties and expertly described.

Antiquities of the Irish Countryside by Seán P Ó Ríordáin. Archaeological remains found in Ireland. Methuen, London, 1942.

Ireland in Pre-History by Michael Herity and George Eogan. Routledge, London, 1976. The ancient past of Ireland.

Irish Castles by Harold G. Leask. Dundalgan Press, Dundalk, 1964. A description of the variety of ruined castles that reflect the state of society in the middle ages.

An Atlas of Irish History by Ruth Dudley Edwards. Methuen, London, 1973. Irish history from the Viking Invasions onward, seen from a practical point of view, with sketch maps and charts.

Irish Folk Ways, by Estyn Evans. Routledge, London, 1953. The tools and utensils of the Irish cottage and countryside, with their regional differences.

The Irish sketch-book by W. M. Thackeray 1843. An account of journeys in Ireland by the famous English novelist. Amusing and well written, but looking on the Irish yokels, as practically every English writer did.

The Aran Islands by J. M. Synge. 1906. Synge developed his literary language from Aran speech and based his plays on what he experienced in Aran.

Oileán Árann (The Arran Islands) by Leo Daly. Albertine Kennedy, Swinford, county Mayo. Do not let the typographical errors in this book detract from your reading. It is an excellent book on its subject.

A History of Ireland by Edmund Curtis. Methuen, 1964.

The Yeats Country Sheelagh Kirby. Methuen, 1962. Those parts of the west that so delighted the poet and provided the basis for his poems and plays.

Coole by Lady Augusta Gregory. Dolmen Press, Dublin 1972. A handsome limited edition. A description of the house in county Clare known to many Irish writers who were guests there, by its last owner.

The People of Ireland by Colman Doyle, the Mercier Press, Cork, 1971. Photographs of Irish people of many types.

My Wallet of Photographs by J. M. Synge. Dolmen Press, 1971. J. M. Synge, the playwright, used a box camera to snap the country people of the mainland and of the Aran Islands.

Songs of the Irish compiled by Donal O Sullivan. Browne Nolan Dublin, 1968. Irish folk music and poetry with English verse translations.

Connacht by Seán Jennett. Faber, London, 1970. A modern journey round the ancient province of Connacht, which includes the west of Ireland.

Index

Aasleagh, 102, 103
Abbeyknockmoy, 41
Achill Island, 107–9
Achill Sound, 107
Achree, Loch, 131
Aran Islands, 19, 55–63, *plate* 4
Ashford castle, 44, 45–6
Athlone, 26
Aughananure castle, 49, *plate* 6
Aughrim, 27
Aughris Head, 131

Ballina, 120, 123, 129
Ballinasloe, 26
Ballinrobe, 127
Ballintubber abbey, 127, *plate* 26
Balleycastle, 96, 119–20
Ballyconneely, 91
Ballymote, 141
Ballynahinch, 3, 65, 69, 70
Ballysodare, 131–2
Bangor Erris, 109, 115
Belderg, 115, 116
Belmullet, 109, 114
Benwee Head, 115
Bertraboy Bay, 90, *plate* 21
Blacksod Bay, 109, 113
Boru, Brian, 6, 8
Boycott, Captain, 128
Brannock Islands, 19, 55
Brendan, St, 28, 63, 110
Bunratty castle, 8–9
Burren, the, 4, 6, 16, 25, 37–8
Burrishoole abbey, 107

Caherballykinvarga, 17
Cairns, 134, 136, 139
Carraigahooley castle, 106–7

Carrigaholt, 3, 23
Carrowkeel, 141
Carrowmore, 135, *plate* 24
Castlebar, 121, 126–7
Caves, 46, 117–18
Claddagh, the, 54
Claregalway, 41
Clare Island, 93, 95, 104
Claremorris, 142
Classiebawn castle, 140
Cleggan, 95
Clew Bay, 104–5, 107
Clifden, 91–2
Clocháns, 62, 96, 139
Clonbur, 46
Clonfert, 28
Clontuskert abbey, 27–8
Collooney, 140–41
Colman, St, 35, 36
Columcille, St, 137–8
Coney Island, 133
Cong, 42–6, *plate* 5
Conn, Loch, 123, 124
Connemara, 4, 69–102; pony show, 92
Coole, 33–5
Corcomroe, 38
Corraun peninsula, 107
Corrib, Loch, 40–41, 47, 48–9, 66, 127,
    plate 2
Costelloe, 66–7
Cottage dwellings, 57, 65, 96, 97, 119–20,
    plates 9–12
Craiganowen, 11–12
Crannógs, 11, 31
Cratloe Woods, 8, 9
Creevelea friary, 136
Creevykeel, 139
Croagh Patrick, 4, 104–5, 127, *plate* 13

Cromwell, Oliver, 6, 27, 28, 37
Cross, co. Clare, 21-2
Cross Abbey, co. Mayo, 109-10
Cuchulainn, legend of, 22-3
Currachs, 18, 20, 59-60, 63, 116

Dalcassians, 6-7, 8
de Clare family, 9, 14, 15
Derg, Loch, 7, 26, 30
Derryhiveney castle, 30
Diarmuid and Gráinne, legend of, 19, 22, 139-40
Dog's Bay, 91
Doonbristy, 117, 118, *plate* 15
Doon castle, 93
Dooney Rock, 135
Doonferry, 116-17
Downpatrick Head, 115, 116-19
Dromohair, 121, 136
Dromoland castle 10
Dromore West, 131
Drumacoo, 38-9
Drumcliff, 137, 138
Dun Aengus, 60-61, *plate* 7
Duvillaun Mór, 113
Dysert O Déa, 14-15

Éanna, St, 61-2, 63
Easky, Loch, 131
Ennis, 13-14
Enniscrone (Inishcrone), 129, 130, *plate* 25
Ennistimon, 17-18
Erris, 3, 109
Errisbeag mountain, 90-1
Erris Head, 115

Fallmore, 109, 113
Farmhouse accommodation, 93-5
Fergus, River, 13
Finian, St, 137
Firbis family, 130, 131
Flannan, St, 7
Folk park, Bunratty, 9
Forts, 11-12, 17, 60-61, 109
Foynes, 10

Gaelic, 2-3, 4, 57, 58, 89, 143-4
Galway, city, 40, 50-54
Gill, Loch, 132, 135-7
Glencar, 137

Gleniff, 139
Gore-Booth family, 138
Gort, 35-7
Gorteen Bay, 91
Gorumna Island, 67-8
Gregory, Lady Augusta,3, 33-4, 38
Guinness family, 43, 45

Hanly, Ellen, 24-5
Headford, 42
Henry, Paul, 48, 97
High crosses, 8, 14, 16-17, 41, 138
High Island, 96
Holiday cottages, 57-8, 65, 96, 97, 119-20
Humbert, General, 120-21, 126, 140

Iar-Chonnact, 3, 64-8
Inisfree, 135
Inishbofin, 95
Inishcrone (Enniscrone), 129, 130, *plate* 25
Inisheer, *see* Aran Islands
Inishglora, 109, 110, 113
Inishkea, 111-13
Inishmaan, *see* Aran Islands
Inishmore, *see* Aran Islands
Inishmurray, 138-9
Inishturbot, 93
Irish language, *see* Gaelic

Joyce's Country, 3, 43, 46, 47

Keel, 107, 108
Keem Bay, 107, 108, 109
Keshcorran, 141
Kilconnell friary, 26-7
Kildavnet castle, 107-8, *plate* 23
Kilfenora, 16-17
Kilkee, 21
Kilkieran, 88-9
Killadoon, 104
Killala, 121-2
Killala Bay, 120-22, 129
Killaloe, 6, 7-8
Killary Harbour, 100-102, 103
Killaspugbrón, 123-4
Killeany, 56, 61-2
Killeen, 104
Kilmacduagh, 35-6
Kilronan, 56, 57
Kilrush, 24

Kincora palace, 8
Kinvara, 37-8
Knappogue castle, 12
Knock, 141-2
Knocknarea, 131-2, 134-5
Kylemore abbey, 98

Lacken Bay, 120
Lahinch, 18
Leamaneh castle, 15-16
Leenaun, 102
Letterbreckaun, 47, 68, 99
Letterfrack, 98
Lír, children of (legend), 110-11
Liscannor, 18-19
Lisdoonvara, 18
Lissadell, 138
Lissoughter, 69
Loch Cutra castle, 36-7
Longford House, 131
Loop Head, 3, 21-5
Loughmask House, 128
Loughrea, 31-2
Louisburgh, 104
Lynch family, 50, 52-3
Lynch's Castle, 52, *plate* 3

Maam Cross, 47, 48, 68
Mac Dara, St, 89
Mac Donnell family, 130
Mac Mahon family, 14, 23
Mac Murrough, Dermot, 136
Mac Namara family, 12
Magheranrush, 136
Mal Bay, 22-3
Mallaranny, 107
Manorhamilton, 137
Markree, 141
Martin, 'Humanity Dick', 69-70
Martin family, 49, 50, 65, 69-70
Martyn, Edward, 33, 38
Mask, Loch, 42, 127
Maumtrasna mountain, 46, 127
Maumturk mountains, 4, 47, 68, 99, 102
Menlough, 41
Misgain Méabh, 132, 134
Moher, Cliffs of, 6, 19
Moneen, 22
Moore, George, 127
Moore, John, 126

Moore, Thomas, 110-11, 136
Moyne abbey, 122-3
Mullaghmore, 140
Mullet peninsula, 109-15
Murrisk, 3, 105
Mweelrea mountains, 4, 97, 102, 103

Nafooey, Loch, 46, *plate* 8
Neale, 127-8
Nephin mountain, 94, 124
Newport, 106

O Brien, Conor, 16
O Brien, Cornelius, 18-19
O Brien family, 6-7, 9, 10, 13, 15, 23, 38
O Connell, Daniel, 13
O Connor family, 41, 43
O Donnell family, 137-8
O Flaherty family, 40, 49, 50, 69, 93, 97
O Madden family, 30, 31
O Malley, Grace, 95, 104, 107
O Rourke family, 136
Oughterard, 48, 66

Pallas castle, 31
Parke's castle, 136, *plate* 18
Patrick, St, 104, 106, 117-18, 122, 127, 133-4
Pearse, Patrick, 88
Peat, *see* turf
Pietà at Strade, 124-6, *plate* 28
Pigeon Hole (cave), 46
Pollnashantinny (cave), 118
Portacloy, 115, 116
Portumna, 30-31
Poteen, 67-8
Punchbowl, the, 37

Quilty, 20
Quin abbey, 12-13

Rathfran abbey, 121
Ring forts, 11-12
Rockfleet castle, 106-7
Roslee, 130
Rosserk abbey, 123
Rosses Point, 140
Roughan, 15

Roundstone, 90, *plate* 22
Round towers, 14, 20, 36, 106, 121–2

St Mac Dara's Island, 89–90
Salruck, 100–101
Salthill, 64
Scattery Island, 24
Screeb Lodge, 68, 70
Seaweed, use of, 20, 88–9, 90, *plate* 21
Senan, St, 24
Shannon, River, 1–2, 6, 7, 8, 24, 26
Shannon Airport, 9–10
Shaw, George Bernard, 34, 38
Skreen, 131
Slieve Auchtys, 30
Slieve Callan, 19
Slieve Gamph, 131
Sligo, town, 3, 129, 132–3, 135, 140,
    plate 16
Somerville and Ross (novelists), 49, 97
Spanish Point, 19–20
Spiddal, 3, 65
Srahmore, 106
Steele, Tom, 13
Strade, 124–6, *plates* 27, 28
Strandhill, 134

Synge, John Millington, 3, 34, 55, 120,
    125

Táin Bo Cuailgne, legend of, 134
Tau Cross of Killinaboy, 15
Thoor Ballylee, 34–5, *plate* 1
Tower-houses, 12, 29–30
'Tribes of Galway', 50–51
Tuam, 41
Tullira castle, 33
Tully, 65–6
Tully Cross, 96, 97, 98
Turbot Island (Inishturbot), 93
Turf, use of, 58, 66, 70, 87–8, *plate* 17
Turoe stone, the, 32–3
Twelve Bens mountains, 4, 69, 99

Westport, 105–6
Wilde, Oscar, 42
Wilde, Sir William, 42, 128

Yeats, Jack B., 32, 34, 133
Yeats, William Butler, 33–4, 34–5, 38,
    121, 132, 133, 135–6, 137, 138, 140
Youth hostels, 69, 101, 115